W9-CKC-535

THE BOOK OF

— OF —

Fascinating

CHRISTIAN

FACTS

ROBERT FLOOD

ACCENT BOOKS
Denver, CO 80215

ACCENT BOOKS

A division of Accent Publications, Inc.
12100 West Sixth Avenue
P.O. Box 15337
Denver, Colorado 80215

Copyright©1985 Accent Publications, Inc.
Printed in the United States of America

All rights reserved. No portion of this book may be reproduced in any form
without the written permission of the publishers, with the exception of brief
excerpts in magazine reviews.

Library of Congress Catalog Number 84-071633

ISBN 0-89636-145-4

Contents

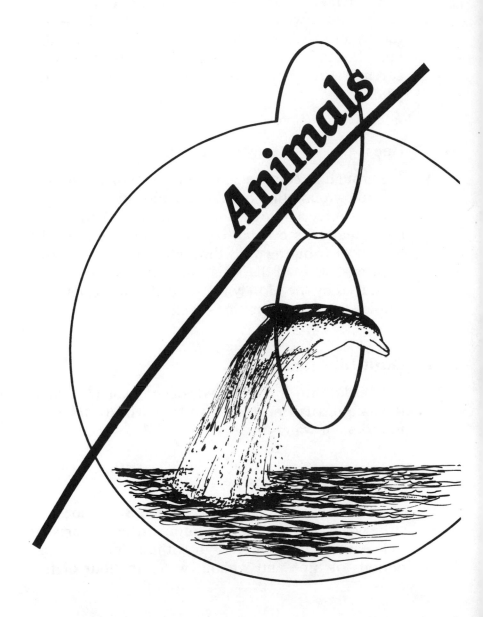

Animals

Back to the Desert

The Israel Nature Reserve Authority released eight onagers—the wild asses mentioned in the Bible—into the Negev Desert in order to revive this animal in that land. It is the first time a species of Bible-era animals, carefully bred in captivity, has been returned to the wild.

Bees

Through a complex, figure-eight dance, one bee describes to another bee the exact location of a good nectar source a mile or more away. The ingenious bee also creates its own air-conditioning system in the hive by distributing water through it and then fanning its wings. "City of the Bees," an award-winning film produced by the Moody Institute of Science, tells the whole story in fascinating detail.

Built-In Sonar

The dolphin has a God-designed "sonar system" that enables it to locate food and avoid obstacles in the murkiest of waters.

Camel's Hump

The camel, often mentioned in the Bible, does not store water in its hump. The hump, instead, stores fat that permits the camel to go without food for long periods of time and without water for four or five days.

Dinosaur Tracks

Dinosaur tracks and human footprints found fossilized in the same rock in the Paluxy River bed near Glen Rose, Texas, provide strong evidence that mankind and dinosaurs lived at the same time. Yet evolutionists put man and dinosaurs millions of years apart.

Diving Spider

The diving spider, or Argyroneta, lives under water but does not drown. It ascends to the water's surface, catches a bubble of air on its hairy abdomen, and breathes air from the bubble while it constructs a silk diving bell. It then brings down more air bubbles to fill the bell. In this underwater home, the spider lives, mates, and rears its young. The process has been photographed by the Moody Institute of Science in its film, "Prior Claim."

Horse and Buggy Traffic

Amish folk, by Biblical conviction, still prefer the simple life. In Millersberg, Ohio, the business district has installed long hitching rails to which Amish customers tie their horses while they shop. The population of Millersburg is about 3,000.

Long-Distance Swimmers

The salmon are remarkable long-distance swimmers with uncanny senses of direction. They will swim as far as 3,000 miles to spawn in the same streams in which they were hatched.

Spitting Fish

The archer fish, or "spitting fish," can knock insects off overhanging branches into water. Its aim is even accurate enough to knock down an insect in flight. This means the fish must judge the height, direction, and speed of the target and the speed and trajectory of the missile that it fires. The fish must also lead its target and allow for refraction of light rays in water. Yet the fish rarely misses.

Talking Fish

Fish can "talk," or make sounds, even though they have no lungs, larynx or vocal cords. (You can hear fish "talking" through a microphone in the Moody Institute of Science film, "Voice of the Deep.")

The Eagle

When the bald eagle was adopted as America's national bird in 1782, Benjamin Franklin did not care for the choice. Thinking the bald eagle had a "bad moral character," Franklin opted, instead, for the turkey. The Bible, however, describes the bald eagle as swift (II Samuel 1:23) and superb in flight. Most Americans have been grateful that the eagle was chosen over the turkey, and take pride today in its lofty, noble appearance.

The Mosquito

The mosquito, whose wings vibrate an incredible 600 strokes per second, lives about 30 days. Only the female mosquito bites. A mosquito cannot see in the dark, but its antennae can detect body heat and skin moisture.

The Ostrich

The largest of all living birds, the ostrich is a poor mother, notes the prophet Job (Job 39:14-16). She often forgets where she lays her eggs and steps on some of them or leaves one for a wild animal to crush or devour. Nor does she show much motherly love.

Job points out, however, that the ostrich can outrun a horse and rider. And God turns even her stupidity to her own good. The eggs that she fails to cover in the sand, when later crushed, provide food for her young.

Buildings

Brimstone Corner

The Park Street Church of Boston was built in 1810 on the site of the town granary where the sails for the frigate "Constitution" ("Old Ironsides") were made. The site became known as "Brimstone Corner," not because of fire and brimstone in the pulpit, but because powder was stored in the crypt of Park Street Church for use in the War of 1812.

C.S. Lewis Landmark

A group of evangelical Christians, some from America, are seeking to buy the Oxford, England, home of the late author C. S. Lewis, in order to restore the house and furnish it with Lewis memorabilia.

The effort to buy the Kilns, as the Lewis property is known, has been spearheaded by Robert P. Cording, president of Omega Films.

The Wheaton College (Illinois) library contains a display of C. S. Lewis items, including some of his original manuscripts and a wardrobe from his boyhood home in Belfast, Ireland. One of C. S. Lewis's most popular classics is *The Lion, the Witch and the Wardrobe*. Lewis is also known for his apologetics of the Christian faith in such books as *The Screwtape Letters, Mere Christianity*, etc.

Chapel of Transfiguration

Some call the Chapel of Transfiguration "the most photographed chapel" in the United States. It stands against the majestic backdrop of the Wyoming Grand Tetons.

Church: A Soft Drink Bottling Plant?

Jerry Falwell started his church in Lynchburg, Virginia, in an old soft drink bottling plant. Today the church has some 20,000 members.

Church of the Presidents

St. John's Church, built in 1816 in lower Manhattan's Lafayette Square, and now dwarfed by the buildings around it, has often been called the "Church of the Presidents." Every President since James Madison has visited it.

Ferrin Hall

Ferrin Hall, a main building on the campus of Barrington College, an evangelical school in Rhode Island, was once a mansion that contained 65 rooms and 28 baths.

Jerusalem Gate

The "Golden Gate" in Jerusalem's East Wall stands on the foundation stones of the portal that Jesus triumphantly entered a few days before he was crucified.

Six hundred years earlier, the prophet Ezekiel had prophesied that the Messiah would enter through this gate. But, Ezekiel 44:2 says that the gate would be closed:

"Then said the Lord unto me, This gate shall be shut, it shall not be opened, and no man shall enter in by it; because the Lord, the God of Israel, hath entered in by it, therefore it shall be shut."

For centuries much of this prophecy had little meaning. But in 1543, Sultan Suleiman the Magnificent did a strange thing. He restored the gate with its arches and ornaments. Then, because the road from the Kidron Valley up to the gate had deteriorated, he immediately had the gate walled up with blocks of stone. It still remains sealed.

John Loizeaux

In February 1982, John Loizeaux, whose family founded Loizeaux Christian books, blew up the historic Cornhusker Hotel in Lincoln, Nebraska. The same month he also dynamited a 21-story building in Seattle.

Loizeaux was not jailed as a terrorist. Firms paid him to do what he did. John Loizeaux happens to be one of the world's foremost demolition experts.

Library of Congress

Scriptural quotations are inscribed on the walls in the Library of Congress. The edifice, which has some 340 miles of shelves, contains a 1455 edition of the Gutenberg Bible.

Little Brown Church in the Vale

Does the "Little Brown Church in the Vale" actually exist, or was it only the figment of a hymnwriter's imagination? Both are true.

The church is in Nashua, Iowa. Schoolteacher

William Pitt, passing through town in a stagecoach in 1857, spotted a picturesque grove of trees and imagined a brown frame church in the setting. Back home in Wisconsin, Pitt wrote the hymn that later became famous and put it in a drawer where it lay forgotten.

Years later, when Pitt returned to Nashua to teach music, he was stunned. By coincidence, a tiny congregation was building a little brown frame church in the grove! The vision of his imagination had become reality. Pitt told his story to the townspeople and he and his music class sang his song at the church's dedication.

Eventually the Weatherwax Brothers, a quartet, discovered the obscure hymn and made it nationally famous over early-day radio. Today the "Little Brown Church in the Vale" attracts some 150,000 visitors a year. Every year, on the first Sunday in August, couples who were married in the little chapel 50 years earlier return to renew their vows.

Norwegian Chapel-in-the-Hills

More than a half-million people have visited the unique "Stavkirke" chapel near Rapid City, South Dakota. Built in 1969, the chapel is an exact copy of the famous 800-year-old Borgund Church in Norway. A pastor conducts half-hour vesper services every evening at 8 during summer months in the chapel.

Oldest Baptist Church in America

The oldest Baptist church in America stands in Providence, Rhode Island. Founded in 1638 by Roger

15

Williams, the church has existed for more than 350 years.

Not coincidentally, the oldest synagogue in America is located in the same city. The climate of religious freedom that Williams and other Baptists established also attracted an early Jewish settlement.

St. John the Divine

The Cathedral of St. John the Divine, the world's largest Gothic cathedral, is not located in Europe. Instead, it is in New York City.

The Crystal Cathedral

The Crystal Cathedral in Garden Grove, California, has 10,661 panes of glass and a sparkling fountain marking the main aisle.

The National Cathedral

The National Cathedral stands on the highest point of land in Washington, D.C. Construction began on the cathedral more than 70 years ago. Famous men buried there include President Woodrow Wilson and former Admiral of the Navy George Dewey.

The Russians Were Here!

On the coast north of San Francisco stands the replica of a Russian Orthodox chapel (the original burned in 1970) built by Russian settlers in 1824. Russian explorers and fur traders hoped to establish what is now California as part of Russia, but in 1841 the Russians finally abandoned such hopes and withdrew.

Thorncrown Chapel

Thorncrown Chapel near Eureka Springs, Arkansas, has been called by some "the most beautiful little chapel in the world." Since it opened on July 10, 1980, it has had more than 750,000 visitors. In 1981, The American Institute of Architects selected it as "one of the 15 best structure designs of the year."

Tudor Castle

Glen Eyrie, international headquarters of The Navigators, a prominent evangelical para-church organization, is located just outside Colorado Springs adjacent to the Garden of the Gods.

The organization's main building, a sixty-seven-room sandstone Tudor-style castle, was built by William Jackson Palmer, the Civil War's youngest general, who moved west to found Colorado Springs and build the Denver and Rio Grande Railroad.

A Gallup Survey

A 1980 survey by pollster George Gallup, Jr., revealed that 95 percent of the Americans polled believe in God. Seventy-one percent believe in life after death. Eighty-four percent believe in heaven. Sixty-seven percent believe in hell.

Another Gallup survey estimated that over 100 million people, a figure up 36 percent from a previous survey, participate in either a Bible study or prayer group. Among those surveyed, 54 percent believed that religion is the solution to the world's problems.

American Broadcasting Company

Word Books, a major Christian publisher headquartered in Waco, Texas, is a subsidiary of the American Broadcasting Company.

Bad News

Among those who identified themselves as Christians in Gallup's survey, only 42 percent knew that Jesus delivered the Sermon on the Mount and only 46 percent were able to name the four Gospels.

Bibles

Thomas Nelson Company of Nashville, Tennessee, is the world's largest publisher of Bibles.

Biblical Coinage

The Roman denarius, or penny, was worth about 20

cents in the time of Christ. This sum amounted to a laborer's wage for one day. The coin was about the size of a U.S. dime, virtually pure silver. It was the principal silver coin of common usage in the Roman world of New Testament times.

Challenges Holiday Inn

For twenty years William Walton served as a top administrator for Holiday Inn. In the late 1970's the hotel chain decided to enter casino and gambling operations against his protest. Because of his integrity, Christian conviction, and respect for the individual, Walton resigned.

Close Company

At least six of the nation's major evangelical magazines have their editorial offices within four blocks of one another: *Christianity Today*, which also publishes *Partnership, Leadership,* and *Campus Life; Christian Life;* and *Christian Reader*. All are located on or just off four-block-long Gundersen Drive, in Wheaton, Illinois.

The offices of *Venture, Dash* and *Trails*, youth magazines published by the Christian Service Brigade and Pioneer Ministries are also just around the corner.

Colonel Sanders: Never Too Late

Colonel Harlan Sanders founded the Kentucky Fried Chicken chain in 1951 at the age of 65—when most people retire. The American operation sold in

1971 for $273 million.

In 1965, at the age of 79, Colonel Sanders went forward in an evangelistic service and accepted the Lord as his personal Savior. "It just seemed like a great burden was lifted off my shoulders," he said. Although his conversion came late in life, Colonel Sanders let Jesus turn his life around.

Communal Colonies

Communal colonies—religious, though not theologically orthodox—founded some of the nation's prominent manufacturing firms.

Oneida, a town in New York state whose name is synonymous with fine silverware and the trade name William Rogers Community Plate, was founded by John Noyes, who established Oneida upon communal concepts that included a "divine organization of society."

Noyes delegated the rearing of children to the community, not to the home. Residents in the area protested so loudly against such breakup of the traditional family that after three decades Noyes finally abandoned the project. A joint stock company in 1880 assumed control of the manufacturing enterprises which the sect had established.

Amana products, even more prominent in today's households than Oneida silverware, originated with the Amana colonies, now one of Iowa's most popular tourist attractions. The Amana settlers migrated from New York state in 1854 to establish seven communal villages between the present cities of Des Moines and Davenport.

The settlers established their own wool mills, furniture factory, wagon shop, meat-smoking plants and other industries which provided the villages with the essentials of life. In true Old World tradition, each member contributed some particular skill handed down from father to son.

These people of European origin, who had left the Old Country because of religious persecution, called their new home Amana, a Biblical term meaning "remain faithful."

Days Inn Founder

On a family vacation in 1968, Cecil Day saw the need for a low-cost, quality motel chain. He tried to put the concept on paper but without success.

Then on a business trip to Virginia, Day awoke early one morning and began to write feverishly. Thirteen hours later he had the entire plan for a motel empire that would eliminate the frills and bring low-cost overnight lodging to millions of American travelers. A devout Christian friend, Tom Fuqua, soon built the first prototype at Georgia's Savannah Beach.

"The ideas were beyond my capabilities," Day later insisted. "It was God's leadership."

Day refused to sell liquor in his motels despite those who insisted that his business could not make a profit without it.

Founder of Quaker Oats

Henry Parsons Crowell, founder of Quaker Oats, served for 40 years (1904-1944) as the Board Chairman of Chicago's Moody Bible Institute.

J.C. Penney's Rebound

Merchant J. C. Penney, son of a Baptist minister, lost a nine million dollar fortune almost overnight in the 1929 stock market crash. The trauma put him in a hospital.

There, early one morning, Penney woke to the distant singing of employees who had gathered in the hospital chapel. "Be not dismayed, whate'er betide," they sang, "God will take care of you." Penney, following the music, slipped into a back row of the chapel.

He left a changed man, regained his health, and rebuilt his chain of department stores across America into an enterprise far greater than the one he had lost. Penney, who adopted the Golden Rule as his business ethic, gave much of his fortune to Christian causes.

Jews for Jesus Ad

When Jews for Jesus, a San Francisco-based organization, placed a full-page evangelistic ad in 25 major metropolitan daily newspapers, some 12,000 people—almost half of them Jewish—answered the ad, wanting to know more about Jesus.

The ad, highlighting the word Y'shua (the Hebrew name for Jesus), ran in nearly 100 metropolitan dailies during the Chanukah season.

The ad appeared nationally in the *Wall Street Journal* and *U.S.A. Today. Time* and *Newsweek* also ran a magazine version although *Newsweek* at first declined, then published the ad a week after it appeared in *Time*. Only *U.S. News & World Report* refused to run it.

Mail Fraud

Postal inspectors receive some 200,000 complaints of mail fraud each year. Nearly one-third come from senior citizens. *Washington Insight*, a newsletter published by the National Association of Evangelicals, reports, "Scams include worthless health insurance plans, underwater land for sale, and vitamin/diet cures for which there is no medical substantiation."

Research shows that cheating costs Americans about $100 billion each year. This includes fraud, shoplifting, loan defaults, and employee theft.

Media Blitz

During the 1983 Christmas season, two and one-half million Americans bought Cabbage Patch dolls.

But four million people requested free copies of the evangelistic book, *Power for Living*, promoted that same season in a national media blitz.

The book includes testimonies of evangelical celebrities like: Charles Colson, entertainer Pat Boone, Dallas Cowboys' head coach Tom Landry, ice skater Janet Lynn, Colorado Senator Bill Armstrong, and baseball star Gary Maddox.

Ads appeared in *TV Guide, U. S. News & World Report, Time, Newsweek,* and *Parade*. Local newspapers and television stations throughout the country also carried ads and commercials.

To obtain the books, respondents called a toll-free

number or sent in a coupon. Tom Turner, president of Frank Vos Advertising Agency, which handled the campaign, said, "There has never been anything quite like the campaign in the advertising world, let alone in the Christian realm."

A foundation established by the late insurance executive, Arthur DeMoss, underwrote the $10 million campaign.

Moody Foundation

The six original trustees of Chicago's Moody Bible Institute included Christians Cyrus H. McCormick, Jr., son of the inventor of the reaper; T. W. Harvey, at one time the greatest retail lumber dealer in the world; and Robert S. Scott, partner in Carson, Pirie, Scott & Co., still one of Chicago's foremost department stores.

Henry Parsons Crowell, founder and Board Chairman of Quaker Oats, was Moody Bible Institute's board president for 40 years.

Moving Down or Moving Up?

R. A. Harlan resigned his position as executive vice-president of ABC Records in New York to become executive vice-president of CRISTA Ministries, a conglomerate of nonprofit Christian organizations headquartered in Seattle.

No Tobacco

With its March 1984 issue, the *Saturday Evening Post*

no longer accepts tobacco advertising. Tobacco advertising forms a major source of revenue received by most secular publications.

Philanthropist

The K in K-Mart got its origin from its founder, Sebastian S. Kresge, who founded the Kresge store chain in Detroit in 1897. The Kresge Foundation, established by the family, is known today for its philanthropic interests, including evangelical causes.

Ray Easter

Ray Easter, vice-president of finance for Radio Corporation of America (RCA), left his position to become director of international finance for World Vision, a Christian relief organization in Monrovia, California.

Record Church Budget

In the largest budget ever adopted by a U. S. church, the First Baptist Church of Dallas, Texas, pledged a record $10 million to the church's 1984 budget.

Religious Paperbacks

Evangelist Dwight L. Moody pioneered religious paperbacks decades before paperbacks became standard format in the book publishing industry. The work he started eventually became Moody Press.

Revealing Survey

A 1982 Licther-Rothman report, which surveyed television network officials, found that almost half of them claim no religious affiliation whatever, and 93 percent say they never attend religious services.

Saturday Evening Post

The *Saturday Evening Post's* born-again religion editor, Robert Silvers, concurrently manages a Post-owned cleanser firm, Bartender's Friend. It is located across the road from the Indianapolis headquarters of the historic magazine that was founded in 1728 by Benjamin Franklin.

Some years ago Silvers, who had no journalism background, persuaded *Post* editor and publisher, Cory Ser Vaas, to do a special issue on Christianity to be published during the Easter season. Silvers volunteered to approach Christian publishers and try to sell the advertising for the issue. It was so successful that the *Post* decided to build religious features, most of them of an evangelical nature, into its regular format.

Stock Exchange

The Zondervan Corporation, owner of more than 80 Christian bookstores in shopping malls across the nation, is the only evangelical firm that sells stock on the New York Stock Exchange.

The Floating Soap

More than 100 years ago, workmen mixing batches of White Soap at Proctor and Gamble took an extra-long lunch hour and allowed a vat of soap to churn too long, beating air into the mixture. When the soap reached the market, delighted customers began to bombard the manufacturer with compliments. The soap, they noted, even floated. By accident the firm had launched a new product but needed a good name for it.

One morning Harley T. Proctor, son of one of the company's founders, sat meditating in church as his pastor read from Psalm 45:8: "All thy garments smell of myrrh, and aloes, and cassia, out of the ivory palaces, whereby they have made thee glad." Suddenly Proctor and Gamble had its new tradename: Ivory Soap.

YMCA/YWCA Origins

Both the YMCA and the YWCA in America originated primarily through the work of evangelist Dwight L. Moody.

Christian Education

Bible Study by Mail

Bible correspondence courses have proved to be an excellent way to reach prisoners with the gospel. The Moody Correspondence School, as one example, enrolls more than 2,000 prisoners.

Big in Texas

Josh McDowell, today the world's foremost campus evangelist, began his rise to prominence in the 1960's on the University of Texas campus, home of more than 30 evangelical movements. He decided that evangelical Christians had as much right to share their message in the marketplace as did the radical leaders of the "free speech" movement.

Chautauqua

The Chautauqua, a movement which took music, culture and education to the towns of America in its early days, was originally founded to train Sunday School teachers. The Chautauqua still has a major conference ground at Chautauqua, New York, near Buffalo.

Christian Law School

Oral Roberts University in Tulsa, Oklahoma, has one of the first Christian law schools now accredited by the American Bar Association. In the early days of America, the study of theology and law were closely linked.

Christmas Sacrifice

About 15,000 students from nearly 900 college and university campuses gave up their Christmas-week vacations in 1983 to attend a Campus Crusade evangelistic strategy session in Kansas City. The largest delegation, 341 students, came from Alabama's Auburn University. The students returned to their schools with the goal of reaching every university campus in the nation with the gospel.

Coed College

Oberlin College, founded in 1833 by evangelist Charles Finney, was the first coeducational institution of higher learning in the United States.

Dartmouth's Beginnings

Dartmouth College was founded in 1754 as a missionary-training school to reach New England Indians with the gospel. Its royal charter, signed by King George III of England, specified the school's intent to Christianize English youth as well as Indians. New England preacher Eleazar Wheelock, the school's founder and a close friend of famed evangelist George Whitefield, secured the charter.

Deaf Students

At Tennessee Temple University in Chattanooga, Tennessee, several hundred deaf students in this school of more than 5,000 hold their own Sunday morning worship service.

First Sunday School in America

The Sunday School originated in England, not in America. Evangelist John Wesley started what some identify as the first Sunday School in America in Savannah, Georgia.

Francis Scott Key

Francis Scott Key, who authored "The Star-Spangled Banner," also helped found the American Sunday School Union in 1824. He served for eighteen years as its vice-president. The movement planted thousands of Sunday Schools across America in the 1800's. Today its name has been changed to the American Missionary Fellowship.

Hall of Fame

Elmer Towns, church-growth specialist, in 1984 was inducted into the Savannah (Georgia) Hall of Fame for his "contributions to Sunday Schools around the world." Towns is a Savannah native.

Heavy Mail

The Sunday School Board of the Southern Baptist Convention, with a postal budget in excess of $3 million annually, is the largest postal customer in Nashville, making Nashville second only to Washington, D.C., in the volume of second-class mail shipped. The volume is so great that the Sunday School Board has its own zip code.

In Macy's Parade

The Marching Flames Band from Jerry Falwell's Liberty Baptist College was one of 12 bands selected from 350 to march in Macy's nationally televised Thanksgiving Day parade.

Internationals

An estimated 400,000 foreign students are enrolled in U.S. universities. International Students, Inc., the foremost evangelical organization reaching out to these students, has its international headquarters and retreat center on the slopes of Cheyenne Mountain near Colorado Springs, Colorado.

Largest Convention

The world's largest Sunday School convention is held each October in Detroit's Cobo Hall. Thousands of Sunday School teachers along with Sunday School suppliers and young people register for the week-long event.

Largest Sunday School

The First Baptist Church of Hammond, Indiana, has registered on some Sundays in excess of 26,000 students in its Sunday School. Buses filled with children arrive in "waves" throughout the day. In some cases, students remain on the buses for class.

McGuffey's Best Seller

More than 120 million copies of *McGuffey's Eclectic Readers* sold between 1836 and 1920. This total put the book in a sales class with the Bible, *Webster's Dictionary*, and the Boy Scout's Manual. The school *Readers* stressed "religion, morality and knowledge" in that order. Author McGuffey was a philosopher and professor at the University of Virginia.

Prayer in German Schools

West Germany not only must allow prayer in its public schools but must provide religious education in any school with 10 or more children from the same religious tradition as that of the parents who request the education.

Presidents

Former President Jimmy Carter regularly taught a Sunday School class at the First Baptist Church of Washington, D.C., during the same time he served as President. Former President Dwight D. Eisenhower taught a Sunday School class during his freshman year as a cadet at West Point.

Princeton's Heritage

Christians established Princeton in 1746 as "The College of New Jersey." It sprang up in part from the impact of the First Great Awakening, a major revival that swept a sixth of New England's early population into evangelical churches.

Every Princeton president until the turn of the 20th century was an evangelical Christian. And Princeton retained its evangelical fervor longer than any other ivy league school.

Protestant School Boom

In the decade of the 70's, enrollment in Protestant schools skyrocketed. Enrollments climbed as much as 50 percent in the Northeast and Midwest. During the same decade, enrollment in public, Catholic, and non-church private schools declined. There are now some 35,000 Christian schools in the United States, with an average of three new ones added each day.

Purchase in San Diego

Campus Crusade has purchased for $28 million more than 5,000 acres in San Diego for a graduate university, a housing development and a high-technology industrial park. The school promises eventually to become a major university with ten schools, including theology, business, law and medicine. Its campus will occupy 1,000 acres.

The other 4,000 acres will become a fashionable planned community of 25,000 homes, designed to perpetually endow the university. It is expected that, in time, the LaJolla Valley project will add 40,000 people to San Diego's population.

The entire package will be managed by University Developments, Inc., a consortium of Campus Crusade and Tecon Realty, a business holding of Clint Murchison, owner of the Dallas Cowboys.

Religion Important

Today far more college students "believe religion is important" than they did five years earlier according to a 1983 Gallup survey on "The Spiritual Climate in America Today." Exactly 50 percent of the students said religion is important as against only 39 percent in 1978.

Rent-a-Campus

Every three years, Christians literally "take over" the University of Illinois campus in Champaign/ Urbana. It happens during the week between Christmas and New Year's when Inter-Varsity Christian Fellowship holds its trienniel student missionary conference. Up to 18,000 students from across the nation, and even from abroad, give up their Christmas vacations to spend the week on campus listening to the challenge of world missions and seeking God's will for their lives.

Roots of Harvard

Harvard University's first presidents and tutors insisted that no true knowledge or wisdom existed without Jesus Christ. The college's earliest "Rules and Precepts," adopted in 1646, stated, "Every one shall consider the main end of his life and studies to know God and Jesus Christ which is eternal life." Students were required to read the Bible twice a day.

Schools at Home

More than two million Americans now teach their children at home. Tests indicate that children who are taught at home for the first two or three grades are more highly motivated, behave better, and learn at least as much as those who go to school.

Findings also suggest that when children taught at home are older, they will be less likely to be swayed by peer pressure.

Seminaries for Texas

More than 5,000 theological students study at two evangelical seminaries in the Dallas-Fort Worth area. Southwestern Baptist Theological Seminary in Fort Worth, the largest seminary in the world, enrolls some 4,000 students. Dallas Theological Seminary enrolls 1,500.

Skydivers

The Grand Rapids School of Bible and Music hosts an annual air show the first weekend in May, complete with flying stunts and skydiving. The show also offers free airplane rides to the public. The event is sponsored by GRSBM's aviation school.

Strategy in Kansas City

Intent on reaching all 3,200 American college campuses for Christ, nearly 15,000 students attended Campus Crusade for Christ's "KC 83" strategy gathering in Kansas City in December 1983 despite subzero temperatures.

They heard the challenge of evangelism, attended seminars, and took the gospel into the streets and homes of Kansas City. The students also distributed food, in conjunction with the Salvation Army, and replaced thousands of smoke alarms in the inner city. In addition, over $1 million was collected from these students in order to take the film, "Jesus," throughout the world.

Thomas Jefferson

The Bible and the *Watts Hymnal* were the principal, if not the only, books used by the first Washington, D.C. public schools. The school board president and chief architect of the system was Thomas Jefferson to whom critics of religion often appeal on issues of church and state.

Visionary

Television evangelist Jerry Falwell has an ultimate goal of 50,000 students for his Liberty Baptist College in Lynchburg, Virginia. He expects an enrollment of 25,000 by the end of the century. Since classes were first held at the college in 1971, it has already grown to an enrollment of nearly 5,000. A 12,000-seat convocation center is now on the drawing boards.

Falwell has challenged the graduates of his college to start 5,000 new churches in North America by the end of the century.

Wandering in the Wilderness

Wheaton (Illinois) College's "Vanguard Program" sends college freshmen into the north woods of Wisconsin for a week of rugged survival training that includes two days totally alone and without food in the wilderness.

Yale's Foundations

Evangelical Christians founded Yale in 1701. One of its most famous presidents, Timothy Dwight, is the author of the hymn, "I Love Thy Church, O Lord."

In the early 1800's a band of Yale evangelical students known as the "Illinois Band," traveled westward to evangelize Illinois. Their spiritual impact on the frontier was significant as they won many to the Lord.

A High Price

Fifty-six men signed the Declaration of Independence. Many of them later paid high prices for their courage and convictions. Nine died during the Revolution. Five were captured by the British and tortured before they died. Twelve saw their homes destroyed by the enemy.

Afloat for the Lord

Ships laden with hundreds of young missionaries now sail both the Pacific and the Atlantic Oceans, docking in the world's major port cities to evangelize continents. The ships not only transport and lodge these young evangelists but also double as floating Bible schools. Two of the ships owned by Operation Mobilization, the "Doulos" (Greek for *servant*) and the "Logos" (Greek for *word*), host some 180,000 people in conferences each year. In port, the main deck of the "Doulos" becomes a huge Christian bookstore as thousands of people come aboard to buy. Over a million people board the two ships each year.

Asian Perspective

Benigno "Ninoy" Aquino, slain in 1983 while opposing the rule of Philippine President Marcos, was a born-again Christian. He had been given a copy of Charles Colson's book, *Born Again*, while imprisoned in 1972. Aquino told Colson the book had changed his life.

Auca Update

In 1957, newspapers in America and abroad headlined the news that five American missionaries had been murdered by savage Indians in the jungles of Ecuador. Auca Indians had attacked the missionaries shortly after they had landed their plane on a remote river sandbar to make contact with the tribe. *Life Magazine* dispatched award-winning photographer Cornell Capa to the scene of the tragedy. Christian young people around the world heard the news and committed themselves to "take the place" of those who had given their lives.

Today all five of the Aucas who killed these missionaries are born-again Christians and are now enthusiastically spreading the gospel among neighboring tribes.

Confederate General

Though Robert E. Lee led the Confederate forces in the Civil War, he did not advocate slavery. As a result of his own personal religious convictions, he had already freed his slaves by the start of the war. After the Civil War, the U.S. government revoked his citizenship, but it was restored posthumously in 1975.

Courage Lost

When Jacob Duche, an Episcopal clergyman in Philadelphia, delivered an eloquent prayer for freedom at the first Continental Congress in 1774, the prayer left many of the delegates highly moved—even weeping. The historic prayer united the Congress in its courage to declare independence from Great Britain.

Three years later, however, when the British captured Philadelphia, Duche wavered between his loyalty to America and his loyalty to the King who was head of the British Anglican Church. Then, as a self-admitted Tory, Duche fled to England, leaving behind the nation whose first Congress he had united and inspired.

Freedom Lost

In early 1984, more than 20,000 Christians were in prisons and labor camps because of their Christian faith. The majority were in socialist and strict Muslim countries. More than 12,000 were imprisoned in the East African Peoples' Republic of Mozambique. Ethiopia, Romania, China and Cuba also put Christians into prison.

Global Expansion

Every day of the year it is estimated that 60,000 people are converted to Christianity. Every week about 1,200 new churches are started throughout the world.

Governments of the People?

Some 197 million people—only about 4 percent of the world's population—consider themselves atheists. Yet governments with atheistic doctrine control half the world's population.

In Cuba

Though Cuban officials quickly confiscate Bibles when they find them, Christianity flourishes in Cuba, say some observers. Of a population of 10 million, about 100,000 are church members. Many more attend worship services in house churches.

In Russia

Evangelical Baptists in the Soviet Union number more than one million. They print Christian literature, hold open-air evangelism meetings, and organize Bible classes. When pastors are arrested, lay leaders come forward to replace them.

"It is the Baptists' very openness, their fervor, their total lack of fear, that strikes dread into the Kremlin," says Michael Bordeaux, leading authority on the status of Christians in Soviet Russia.

In the World

Some 290 million Christians live under communist regimes worldwide.

Jack Lousma

Jack Lousma, commander of the space shuttle Columbia's March, 1982 flight, grew up in the ranks of the Youth for Christ movement. In his 1973 Skylab 3 flight, Lousma flew more than 24 million miles in 59 days and walked for 11 hours in space.

At the time of Lousma's Columbia flight, the recorded testimony of his own personal faith in Jesus

Christ was broadcast into Communist lands· by shortwave radio.

John Hancock

At the time that John Hancock signed the Declaration of Independence in large sweeping strokes, risking both life and fortune, he was one of the richest men in America.

Knott's Berry Farm

In the early 1920's Walter and Cordelia Knott, devout Methodists, bought a berry farm at Buena Park, California, and set up a roadside stand. When the Depression hit, Cordelia turned her home into a bustling dining room and shifted to chicken dinners. Crowds stood in line to enjoy her food. Walter worried about keeping the people occupied while they waited. Eventually he assembled a few attractions to keep waiting families amused.

The rest is history. Knott's Berry Farm became the nation's first amusement park. It still remains one of the largest in the country. And it has never sold alcohol.

Long Distance Witness

Colonel Heath Bottomly, one of America's most famous Viet Nam jet fighter pilots, was led to the Lord during a long-distance phone call with his Christian son, a student at Purdue University in Indiana, more than 9,000 miles away from Viet Nam.

Bottomly had called, in dejection, to tell his son that he was being demoted for downing an enemy plane across the Viet Nam border in violation of orders from President Lyndon Johnson.

Madalyn Murray O'Hair

Atheist Madalyn Murray O'Hair tried to defect to Soviet Russia shortly before she took her school prayer suit to the U.S. Supreme Court in 1963.

William Murray, Madalyn's oldest son who converted to Christianity in 1980 but was raised in Marxism, says his mother was employed by the Communist Party when she began her crusade to remove prayer from public schools 20 years ago.

Miracle at Dunkirk

In May 1940, Adolph Hitler's German panzer divisions were pushing nearly one-half million British and French troops toward the sea at Dunkirk in what appeared to be certain annihilation.

"Nothing but a miracle can save (us) now," wrote British Lieutenant-General Alan Brooke in his diary.

What followed was a series of "miracles." Hitler suddenly called off his tanks in order to save them for a drive on Paris. The Nazi commanders were furious because Hitler's unpredictable move gave Allied forces time to fortify Dunkirk and plan an escape across the English Channel. But the British predicted that, even with the best of luck, they would save only 30,000-40,000 men. The Nazis, it appeared, would surely destroy them by air.

As the rescue began, thick black smoke from nearby oil refineries which Germans had bombed closed in on Dunkirk Beach. The wind had shifted in the right direction to conceal the thousands of men trying to make their escape into boats along the shore. The Germans waited helplessly, but were sure they would still get their chance for a grand-scale massacre.

Then the fog closed in and stayed for the better part of nine days. The British had sent out a distress call for English boats of all kinds to aid in the rescue. Naval vessels and destroyers alone could not handle such a mass evacuation. Civilians rushed to the scene with an armada of pleasure yachts and decrepit fishing boats.

The normally rough seas at Dunkirk would have smashed these craft against the rocks. But in a strange and unusual phenomenon, the English Channel stayed calm like a millpond for days. The Germans had few chances to spread their deadly fire from the air. Incredibly, by June 4, over 338,000 troops had been evacuated to England. The nation rejoiced.

But behind the "miracle" lay another factor, perhaps the most significant of all. In late May, in the face of the Dunkirk crisis, England's King George VI had announced a national day of prayer. "At this humble hour," he said, "we turn, as our fathers before us have turned in all times of trial, to God the Most High . . . . Let us with one heart and soul humbly but confidently commit our cause to God."

Mission Field: Grand Canyon

The Arizona-based United Indian Mission has assigned missionaries to such remote places as the bottom of the Grand Canyon. Members of the Havasupai tribe live on the floor of the canyon, a place accessible only by steep descent on muleback.

Missionary Martyrs

From the time of the 1900 Boxer Rebellion to the 1948 Communist takeover, eight graduates of Chicago's Moody Bible Institute died as missionary martyrs in China. Most famous of these were John and Betty Stam.

In December 1934, they were captured in Tsingtech and held ransom by communists for $20,000—a large sum in those days. Their captors decided to kill the Stams' three-month-old baby, Helen Priscilla, who kept crying because of the noise and rifle fire. But an old farmer, a non-Christian just released from prison, offered his life in exchange for that of the baby. In front of the Stams, the communists chopped the farmer to pieces.

Two days later the Stams, aged 26 and 27, were publicly beheaded. Their baby, hidden in a house, was found unharmed thirty hours later by a Chinese Christian and smuggled out of danger. The Stam daughter grew up to become a Christian missionary like her martyred parents.

No Job Shortage

Intercristo, a national job referral service for Christians, reports 7,000 openings are available for short-term overseas missionaries. Intercristo employs the computer to match the skills and backgrounds of those who utilize its services with openings for

Christian service both at home and abroad.

"No" to the King

The Wright brothers' Christian upbringing, along with the culture of the day, gave them a strong respect for the Lord's day. On one occasion the King of Spain asked the two men to take him aloft in their marvelous new invention, the "flying machine." The brothers declined. It was Sunday.

Prayer in the Capital

On April 29, 1980, a half-million Christians gathered in Washington, D.C. to fast and pray for America. The gigantic prayer meeting lasted 11 hours and was sponsored in part by Intercessors for America.

Sea Burial

Adoniram Judson, famous Baptist missionary to India, was buried at sea. He died in 1850, in frail health, while sailing for the Isle of France.

The Surgeon General

Dr. C. Everett Koop, Surgeon General of the United States, was once president of the Christian Medical Society and still serves on its board. The CMS has a vigorous evangelical outreach to those in the medical profession.

Today

The Salvation Army forfeited $4.4 million in social service contracts with the city of New York when, in early 1984, the Army refused to comply with the mayor's executive order about nondiscrimination against homosexuals in employment practices. The Salvation Army was the only religious agency that refused to sign the revised city contracts.

World Missions Budget

North America's support of Protestant missions now totals an estimated one billion dollars a year.

Wrong Man

Georgi Vins, Russian Baptist pastor exiled to the United States, says that one of nine charges brought against him by the Soviet Union was that he wrote the 23rd Psalm.

The Soviets found a copy of the Psalm among his possessions, verified the handwriting as his, and concluded that he was the author. When Vins tried to tell his accusers that King David had penned the words 3,000 years ago, the Russian court refused to believe him.

Youth With a Mission

Youth With a Mission (YWAM), which owns a 11,695-ton ship, *Anastasis*, sends some 10,000 young people into the nations of the world each year as short-term missionaries.

Discoveries and Inventions

Computer Bible Translation

Computers have vastly speeded up the process of Bible translation. In some cases they have saved linguists years of work. Missionary translators now take portable computers with them into the jungles.

Cyrus McCormick

Cyrus McCormick, who in 1831 invented the reaper and later founded the International Harvester Company, was an outspoken lay theologian and Christian. His son, Cyrus McCormick, Jr., was one of the original trustees of Chicago's Moody Bible Institute.

Dead Sea Scrolls

The now famous Dead Sea Scrolls were discovered by a Bedouin shepherd boy in 1948 in a cave near Qumran, close to the Dead Sea. The Scrolls have established that the present Old Testament, though passed down through the centuries, is essentially the same text as the ancient one found by the shepherd.

The Scrolls are major evidence that the modern Bible is an accurate copy of the words that God inspired his prophets and leaders to write.

On display at Hebrew University in Jerusalem, the Scrolls are protected under glass, and the exhibit can be lowered into the ground at night or in the event of enemy attack.

Earthmoving Machines

Christian philanthropist R.G. LeTourneau built the world's largest earthmoving equipment and founded LeTourneau College, a Christian school in Longview, Texas. He was a man of great spiritual stature who could "move mountains" both with his faith and his heavy equipment.

Ebla

The buried city of Ebla, in northern Syria, was discovered in 1964. Careful analysis revealed that it was the seat of a mighty empire that had flourished around 2400 B.C.

Ebla excites Bible scholars because 16,000 cuneiform tablets found in Ebla's ancient library contain references to numerous people and places mentioned in the Bible.

Among them are the cities of Sodom and Gomorrah. Some Bible critics had long insisted that cities like these never existed.

Ezekiel Airship

In the little town of Pittsburg, Texas, local residents insist that a flying machine invented by a Baptist pastor beat the Wright Brothers into the air by a full year. Called the "Ezekiel Airship," the Texas machine reportedly lifted about ten feet off the ground, flew more than 160 feet, then landed in a pasture. Today a roadside plaque marks the "historic" site.

Hideaway Fishing Rod

Everett Horton of Connecticut invented the telescoping fishing rod in 1886 because early Connecticut law prohibited fishing on the Sabbath. Horton wanted a fishing rod he could hide when he went fishing on Sundays.

MARC

At the Missions Advanced Research Center (MARC) in Pasadena, California, missionary strategists have been using computers for more than a decade to plan strategies for world evangelization.

Mount Ebal

Archaeologist Adam Zartell is convinced he has uncovered an altar built by Moses and Joshua on Mount Ebal. Zartell, who began digging at the mountain site on the West Bank in 1982, says the altar dates from the 12th century B.C., and he believes it was built during the Exodus.

Rickshaw

An American evangelical invented the rickshaw. He was Reverend Jonathan Scobie, a Baptist minister who lived in Yokohama, Japan, around 1870.

Samuel Morse

Samuel F. B. Morse was the son of the Rev. Jedediah Morse, one of New England's most outspoken early evangelical preachers. In 1794, Jedediah wrote the first geography book published in the United States (*Geography Made Easy*) and became known as the "father of American geography."

Son Samuel was not only an inventor but an accomplished artist. A Samuel Morse painting recently sold for a record $8 million.

In 1844 Morse telegraphed his historic message, "What hath God wrought" (or, "See what God has done"), from Washington, D.C. to Baltimore. The words are taken from Numbers 23:23.

3-D Camera

Jerry Nims, an evangelical Christian, blazed a trail in photographic technology with his invention of the Nimslo 3-D camera. Though nearly bankrupt in 1977, Nims, because of a market breakthrough, had propelled his company's value to $450 million by 1982.

Nims gives generously to evangelical causes, including programs to help the poor in Atlanta and Denver, and helps persecuted Christians of Eastern Europe.

The Exodus?

Archaeologists have uncovered a string of settlements in the Sinai Desert that they believe may be related to the exodus of the Israelites from Egypt. The towns closely follow the route that the Israelites took.

World's Primitive People

Are all the so-called "primitive" peoples of the world uncivilized people "on the way up," as evolutionists insist? Or are they once-civilized people "on the way down"? Here are some amazing facts to ponder:

The Lacandones: The "primitive" Lacandones of Chiapas, Mexico are descendants of the once great Mayans whose civilization peaked about the time Jesus walked on earth. The Mayans once had hundreds of cities spread across Central America. Accomplished astronomers and architects, they developed the concept of "zero" at least 1,000 years before Europe did.

Western civilization, in fact, did not have the zero until the Middle Ages, when the Phoenicians brought it into Europe from the Hindus.

The Quechuas: Five million Quechuas are a so-called "primitive" people who live in Peru. Many of them are addicted to cocaine. Yet they descend from the once great Incan civilization. The empire's network of roads included the Royal Road of the Incas that was 3,250 miles long (longer than from San Francisco to New York). The Incan water system lasted for centuries and parts of it are still intact. There is also evidence that, as superb surgeons, the Incas mastered the skill of brain surgery even before the time of Christ!

Wright Brothers

The Wright brothers, Wilbur and Orville, were sons of a bishop in the Evangelical Church. On December 17, 1903, the brothers kept their "flying machine" aloft 12 seconds over the sands of Kitty Hawk, North Carolina, and ushered in the era of flight.

The brothers made four flights that famous day. The first attempt took them only 120 feet, less than the distance (195 feet) between the wingtips of a Boeing 747. But by the end of the day they had stretched the distance to 852 feet and stayed aloft 59 seconds.

Evangelism

"Go ye into all the world..."

Ballplayer Turned Evangelist

Billy Sunday, America's most famous evangelist of the early 20th century, once pitched for the Chicago White Stockings (the name was changed to Chicago White Sox in 1911). Fans labeled Sunday the only man who could round the diamond, touching every base, in 14 seconds.

Sunday left professional ball to become a full-time evangelist. By the end of his career, which spanned a quarter century, Sunday had preached 20,000 times. Over one million people, it is said, gave their hearts to God during his campaigns.

Beach Evangelism

Nearly 5,000 college and university students spend their yearly spring breaks spreading the gospel to their peers on the sands at Daytona Beach, Florida.

The annual outreach is organized by Campus Crusade for Christ. Inter-Varsity Christian Fellowship, another para-church campus movement, also sends hundreds of students to Fort Lauderdale, Florida, to share the gospel each year during spring break.

Billy Graham's Roots

Evangelist Billy Graham wanted to be a professional ballplayer, and he did play a few semi-pro games for $10-15 each.

Billy practiced his earliest sermons by preaching alone from a stump in the Florida swamps.

The house in Charlotte, North Carolina, where Billy Graham was born, has now become the site of a towering IBM building. Thoughtfully, IBM has mounted a marker showing people the birth site of this world-renowned evangelist.

Borden of Yale

The famous "Borden of Yale" gave one million dollars to the cause of world missions before his death while still in his 20's.

Cattle on a Thousand Hills

Steer, Inc., a Christian organization headquartered in Bismarck, North Dakota, involves Christian ranchers in raising cattle for missions. In the past two decades, ranchers have channeled more than a million dollars into the mission field.

Steer, Inc. has its own brand and an annual round-up. Its Biblical motto comes from Psalm 50:10: "All the beasts of the forests are mine, and the cattle upon a thousand hills."

Child Evangelism

Child Evangelism Fellowship, headquartered in Warrenton, Missouri, reaches more than a half million children a year with the gospel through its outreach programs at state and county fairs.

Christianity Booms

In 1900 only three percent of all Africa was Christian. If Christianity continues to grow at its present rate, 48 percent of the population will be Christian by the turn of the century. Some 85 percent of all school children on the continent attend Christian schools.

Cowboys for Christ

A few decades ago most rodeo cowboys drank heavily and tore up hotels when they came into town for a rodeo. Today many cowboys are turning to the Lord.

The Cowboy Chapter of the Fellowship of Christian Athletes (Cowboys FCA) now has more than 4,000 members from the professional rodeo circuit, amateur and high school rodeos, and the "Little Britches." The Chapter has distributed more than 60,000 copies of the "Cowboy Bible" (New Testament).

Now a new affiliate, Cattlemen for Christ, has been launched.

In some rural areas the Cowboy FCA is the "in" youth movement. A young person who joins for seven dollars a year receives a membership packet that includes: a Cowboy Bible; bumper stickers; window decals; and a monthly newsletter, "Circuit Rider." The common bond of the movement is a love for horses— and the Savior.

D. L. Moody

Shoe salesman Dwight L. Moody abandoned his desire of becoming a millionaire to serve the Lord and live on a personal income of $120 per year. Later the success of the *Moody-Sankey Hymnal*, that became popular because of Moody's great crusades both in

America and the British Isles, generated more than a million dollars in royalties. But neither Moody nor Sankey ever accepted a penny of these royalties. The money went entirely for Christian and philanthropic causes.

Dial-A-Teen

Christian teenagers in Washington, D.C., who several years ago started a Dial-A-Teen counseling service, receive at least 1,000 calls a day. Their work has been cited by President Ronald Reagan.

Generous Givers

Fifty-six percent of all individual contributions in the United States goes toward religious organizations, reports the Chemical Bank Economic Research Department. Religious groups depend on individuals, rather than on corporate contributions, for 98 percent of their funding.

Growing Movement

The Christian Legal Society, an organization comprised of evangelical lawyers, judges, and law school students, now has a membership of more than 4,000 and a vigorous evangelistic outreach on some university campuses. The Society is attempting to return the practice of law to its original Biblical foundations.

Jack Wyrtzen

Jack Wyrtzen's Word of Life camps on Schroon Lake in the New York Adirondacks, has its own island. Reached only by boat, the island is the geographical focus of Word of Life's high school and college camps.

Lawyer Turned Evangelist

Charles Finney, a brilliant young lawyer, as he was becoming successful, bought his first Bible because the law books he studied made frequent references to the Scriptures. At first embarrassed to be seen with the Bible, he hid it under his other textbooks. But once he began to read it, its words brought conviction to his heart.

The day he was converted, he won 24 to the Lord in his town, among them another lawyer and a distiller. Later in Boston, as an evangelist, he saw 50,000 accept the Lord in one week. It is said that Finney's preaching influenced change in one-half million lives.

Finney also designed New York's Broadway Tabernacle, whose pastorate he accepted in 1836, to seat 2,500 people within 80 feet of the preacher.

Netherlands Antilles

In 1971, the Netherlands Antilles released a postage stamp commemorating Trans-World Radio, another Christian-built superpower shortwave outreach that spans the globe.

New England Impact

The first phase of America's Great Awakening lasted for 20 years and saw approximately 40,000 of a population of 300,000 come to Christ in New England alone.

Revivalist Scholar

J. Edwin Orr, the world's leading authority on revivals and awakenings, has four earned doctorates and has written 17 books on revival.

Salvation Army

The Salvation Army, which has earned its reputation primarily in cities, suffered persecution when it first came to the United States from Great Britain in 1880. America was unfriendly and several officers lost their lives from violence. But in 1886 President Grover Cleveland received a delegation of Salvation Army officers and gave the organization his official and personal endorsement. Since then every President has done the same.

Teenager's Vision

The Wycliffe Bible Translators have given over 950 language groups around the world alphabets and written forms of their mother tongues. With more than 5,000 missionaries in 40 countries, Wycliffe is the largest evangelical mission in the world.

The work began more than 50 years ago when the

late Cameron Townsend, then 17, set out on foot into Guatemala to sell Spanish Bibles.

One day on the trail he sat down to rest next to a Cakchiquel Indian who blurted out, "Why, if your God is so smart, doesn't He speak our language?"

Still reeling from the remark, Townsend settled down with the tribe and stayed for 15 years. He learned the Cakchiquel culture, ate their food, and mastered their language. Townsend gave them the New Testament, in their own tongue, in 1931. The time he spent there also gave him the basic methodology for teaching others how to translate the many previously unwritten tribal languages of the world.

When Cameron Townsend recently died, he was eulogized by peasants and Presidents worldwide.

The Gospel and the Alcoholic

America's Keswick, a major conference and retreat center near Whiting, New Jersey, has an adjacent rehabilitation center for male alcoholics that dates back to 1897.

William Raws, a dying drunkard set free from the bonds of alcohol by the superior power of the gospel, founded the center to reclaim men like himself. Thousands of men from all walks of life, including doctors, lawyers, university professors, and businessmen, have found their way to Keswick and in hundreds of cases to new, happy, successful lives.

In 1970, William Raws, grandson of the founder and the third generation devoted to this ministry, assumed the overall administration of America's Keswick.

They Changed England

William Wilberforce, an evangelical who served as a member of England's Parliament, is given major credit for abolishment of his nation's slave trade in 1807. The influence of Hannah More, evangelical leader in education, augmented that of Wilberforce. The two greatly improved the morals of England's upper classes. Cockfighting died out, and "dirty" bookstores closed for lack of customers.

Third World Evangelists

Hundreds of evangelists from Third World countries attended the 1983 International Conference for Itinerant Evangelists at Amsterdam. Added to this success, Christian businessmen provided more than $250,000 worth of clothing. These garments were channeled through the Samaritan's Purse, an organization headed by Franklin Graham, son of evangelist Billy Graham.

Tribute to the Superpowers

In 1981, the Ecuadorian government released a series of stamps commemorating the 50th anniversary of Radio HCJB, which broadcasts the gospel to Latin America and around the world. The station's call letters stand for "Herald Christ Jesus' Blessings."

200th Translation

In 1983 the Hanga tribe of Ghana, West Africa, was presented the Wycliffe Bible Translators' 200th complete translation of the New Testament. More than 3,000 language groups throughout the world, however, still have no Bible.

U. S. Landmark

Cary Lott, a freed slave from Virginia, is given the primary credit for planting the gospel in Liberia, Africa. After his conversion, he learned to read, became a Baptist preacher, then went abroad as a missionary in the early 1800's to become the pastor of the first Baptist church in that African nation. The U.S. Government recently declared his birthplace in Charles City, near Richmond, Virginia, a national landmark.

Wealth Passed By

Evangelist Dwight L. Moody gave up a promising career in Chicago's business world to step out on faith without salary and give himself full time to the outreach of the gospel. But he cultivated and maintained his contacts with Chicago's business elite, including Marshall Field, whom he once admitted was perhaps the only man in Chicago that he could not have surpassed in a business enterprise.

When he founded Moody Bible Institute in 1886, D. L. Moody placed on its board two of Chicago's most prominent business citizens, International Harvester's Cyrus McCormick, Jr., son of the reaper's inventor, and Robert S. Scott, partner in Carson, Pirie, Scott, still one of Chicago's most prominent department stores. Both men had strong evangelical convictions.

Wheaton-of-the-West

Colorado Springs, Colorado is now the national headquarters for numerous evangelical organizations, prompting some to call the city the "Wheaton of the West"—a reference to the many Christian organizations headquartered in Wheaton, Illinois, just west of Chicago.

Among the ministries based in Colorado Springs are Young Life Campaign, the Christian Booksellers Association, The Navigators, International Students, Inc., Compassion, and former astronaut Jim Irwin's High Flight Foundation.

Whitefield's Voice

Evangelist George Whitefield had such a booming voice that he could speak to a crowd of 20,000 outdoors, without the need for vocal amplification and still be heard by all.

Benjamin Franklin, one of Whitefield's admirers, thought Whitefield should have a building in which to preach when he came to Philadelphia so Franklin helped Whitefield raise the money for it. The structure later became the first building on the University of Pennsylvania campus.

A statue of evangelist George Whitefield stands on the campus today, honoring his influence in the founding of the University of Pennsylvania.

William Jennings Bryan

In Lincoln, Nebraska the public may tour the home of William Jennings Bryan, the evangelical "Silver-tongued Orator" who delivered his famous "Cross of

Gold" speech at the Democratic National Convention in Chicago in 1896. His home stands next to the William Jennings Bryan Hospital at 4848 Sumner Street.

Bryan was a three-time candidate for President and a tireless critic of Social Darwinism.

World Medical Assistance

The Medical Assistance Program (MAP), an evangelical agency, channels more than $15 million in drugs, medical supplies and equipment to the mission fields of the world each year. Much of this is donated by major pharmaceutical firms.

Yale Scholar

Evangelist Jonathan Edwards, thought to have one of the most brilliant minds in early America, graduated from Yale at age 17. His preaching from Enfield, Massachusetts triggered what became known as America's First Great Awakening. One of every six inhabitants in America at that time was swept into evangelical churches.

Yacht Evangelism

A yacht owned by resort evangelist Terry Lytle cruises Lake Michigan full time, except in winter, ministering to the lake's boat-loving "up and outers."

Meanwhile, when ships dock in Chicago from foreign countries, an evangelist with the Great Lakes Seamen's Mission ensures that sailors receive copies of the Bible printed in their own languages.

Across the Rockies

The first white women to cross the Rockies were Christian missionaries, Narcissa Whitman and Eliza Spaulding. Narcissa and her husband, Marcus, were among more than a dozen missionaries killed by Indians at the mission station near what is now Walla Walla, Washington in 1847.

Air Force Jet Pilot

A Christian housewife, Connie Engel, was the first woman to become a jet pilot in the United States Air Force, when, on November 30, 1976, she soloed in a T-37.

Christopher Columbus

Strong evidence suggests that the Bible and spiritual convictions encouraged Christopher Columbus to set sail for the New World. He once wrote:

> It was the Lord who put into my mind (I could feel His hand upon me) to sail from here to the Indies. All who heard of my project rejected it with laughter, ridiculing me. There is no question that the inspiration was from the Holy Spirit, because He comforted me with rays of marvelous illumination from the Holy Scriptures ... encouraging me continually to press forward....

Columbus wrote a book on the prophecies of Isaiah (later translated from Portuguese) in a day when few laymen knew the Bible. Tradition says that Columbus did not permit his sailors to swear. But there is also evidence that, as Columbus' life unfolded, he allowed "gold and glory" to consume his earlier passion for God. As a result, his later voyages proved disastrous. Columbus lost credibility, and his personal life fell on ill times.

Close Ones

In 1916, Woodrow Wilson carried California by one vote per precinct. And because he won California, he won the Presidency.

In 1948, Lyndon Johnson won his first election to the U. S. Senate by only 87 votes—out of more than 988,000 cast. The Senate gave him the base for his later step into the Presidency.

Explorer Castillo

Mixed motives may have plagued some of the early explorers. Bernard Diaz del Castillo, who explored Florida, once said of his ventures, "We came here to serve God, and also to get rich."

First Presidential Broadcast

Warren G. Harding's dedication of the Francis Scott Key Memorial at Fredericksburg, Maryland on February 8, 1922, was the first Presidential speech broadcast on radio. Fredericksburg was Key's birthplace.

Florence Nightingale

Florence Nightingale saved hundreds of lives in the Crimean War, cleaned up British hospitals, and made nursing a respectable profession. But when honored by Queen Victoria and the British Parliament, Nightingale was uncomfortable. To Florence Nightingale, she had simply answered the call of God upon her life. "Christ is the author of our profession," she said of nursing.

Garfield, the Preacher

James Garfield, the first President to use a telephone, took the Lord Jesus into his life as Savior at a camp meeting and was baptized, at age 17, in the cold waters of the Chagrin River. As a young man he preached frequently from pulpits and once baptized 40 converts during a two-week evangelistic campaign. On one occasion, more than a half century before the famous Scopes trial, Garfield publicly debated an articulate atheist/evolutionist in a series and, according to witnesses, won decisively.

Gerald Ford's Son

Former President Gerald Ford's son, Michael, graduated from an evangelical seminary in Massachusetts while his dad was in office and then entered the ministry. (He is now director of student activities at North Carolina's Wake Forest University.)

Geronimo

Apache Chief Geronimo, who spent years avenging the death of his fellow Apaches at the hands of the white men, eventually became a Christian and was baptized at a Fort Sill, Oklahoma, church in 1903. He died in 1909.

Golden Rule Merchant

The late J. C. Penney, founder of the prominent department store chain bearing his name, was the son of a Primitive Baptist minister who drilled into his son the importance of scrupulous business ethics. Young Jim Penney launched his business with "the Golden Rule" as his basic principle of operation, and soon built his store chain into one of the nation's giants. With the Depression, however, Penney's fortune plummeted, leaving him almost bankrupt. In a hospital one morning he heard employees gathered for morning chapel singing "Be not dismayed, whate're betide, God will take care of you...." Penney slipped quietly into the service. He left a changed man, and soon rebuilt his enterprise into an even greater business empire. Penney gave much of his wealth to Christian and philanthropic causes, and for many years wrote a regular column, "Lines of a Layman," for *Christian Herald* magazine.

Hoover, the Quaker

Herbert Hoover, 31st President of the U. S., is buried only a short distance from the rural Quaker "Meeting House" he attended as a boy in West Branch, Iowa.

During his entire 47 years in government, Hoover gave each of his federal salary checks to charity. As a young man, he had already become independently wealthy.

It's Really True

Southern Baptist Jimmy Carter was the first American President to be born in a hospital.

Jason Lee

A U. S. postage stamp commemorated the establishment of the Oregon Territory. Missionary Jason Lee and his brother, Daniel Lee, pioneered Oregon's Willamette Valley as early as 1834 and established a Methodist mission there.

Lee not only proclaimed the gospel but also the merits of the Willamette Valley. He, more than any other individual, promoted the early settlement of Oregon.

Jedediah Smith

In 1826 Jedediah Smith, Bible-totin' trailblazer and American explorer, became the first white man to cross the Great Salt Lake Desert and the Sierra Nevada Mountains. His daring took him as far as Fort Vancouver in the Pacific Northwest. Jedediah Smith was killed by Comanche Indians near the Cimarron River in southwestern Kansas on May 27, 1831.

John Wesley Powell

John Wesley Powell, the famous American explorer who discovered the Colorado River, once studied at what is now Wheaton College in Illinois and also at Oberlin College in Ohio, founded by evangelist Charles Finney. Powell, son of a circuit-riding preacher, taught science at a Christian school before leaving to explore the West.

In 1869 Powell, who had one arm amputated during the Civil War, put together an 11 man expedition to explore the rapids of the Colorado River and the Grand Canyon where no white man had ventured before. Among the expedition's daring taskforce of geologists, historians, and various scientists were three ministers.

Some of the men later turned back. Indians killed three members of the expedition. Yet those who completed the trip told the world of an unimaginable frontier wilderness and beauty.

What made Powell push on when he might have fled in fear? One biographer put it this way: "He was made by wandering, by hard labor, and by the Bible . . . . "

Jungle Pilot

Pioneer missionary aviatrix Betty Greene was the first pilot to fly for Mission Aviation Fellowship and the first woman pilot to fly over South America's Andes Mountains. Only recently retired, she flew for 34 years. Betty Greene flew missionary supplies over the steep mountain gorges of Borneo's interior as early as 1946.

Leif Ericson

Evidence exists that Columbus did not really discover America. Some scholars argue that Norwegian explorer Leif Ericson reached New England 400 years before Columbus by way of Greenland, Newfoundland, and Labrador.

Leif Ericson was a born-again Christian. His father, Eric the Red, according to legend, established a small settlement in Greenland about 980 A.D. Son Eric returned to Norway for a time and was converted while visiting the court of King Olaf Tryggvason.

When he shared his new faith with his family in Greenland, all but his father also accepted the Lord.

Leif Ericson's mother built Greenland's first chapel. Sixteen churches dotted Greenland's coastline by the 1300's.

Persistent reports reveal that Leif sailed to North America around 1000 A.D., landing in three places, one of them a place he called Vinland.

The remains of nine houses were discovered in 1961 near a small Newfoundland fishing village. Tests of the charcoal in the ember pits dated the houses to about 1000 A.D. The houses themselves reflected not Indian or Eskimo design but Norwegian style.

A smithy, designed to extract iron from nearby deposits, was discovered. The Indians had no such iron extraction process at that time.

"Lemonade Lucy"

Lucy, the wife of President Rutherford B. Hayes, did not serve alcohol nor would she permit tobacco in the

White House. Because of abstinence, she earned the nickname, "Lemonade Lucy."

Lincoln and the Bible

Abraham Lincoln once said, "The Bible . . . contains an immense amount of evidence of its own authenticity. I decided a long time ago that it was less difficult to believe that the Bible was what it claimed to be than to disbelieve it."

Long Time in Prayer

Two United States postage stamps show George Washington kneeling in prayer. One was released in 1928, the other in 1977.

Luther Honored

In 1983, the United States Postal Service issued a commemorative stamp on the 500th Anniversary of Martin Luther's birth.

On Commitment

"Christianity is like the service. You're in it no matter what comes up."
> —John W. Vessy, chairman of
> the Joint Chiefs of Staff.

On National Judgment

"More than a half century ago, while I was still a child, I recall hearing a number of older people offer the following explanation for the great disasters that had befallen Russia: 'Men have forgotten God—that's why all this has happened.'

"Since then I have spent well nigh fifty years working on the history of our Revolution. But if I were asked today to formulate as concisely as possible the main cause of the ruinous Revolution that swallowed up some 60 million of our people, I could not put it more accurately than to repeat: 'Men have forgotten God; that's why all this has happened!'"

—Alexander Solzhenitsyn,
Nobel Prize-winning novelist,
in an address May 10, 1983,
at London's Buckingham Palace.

On Prosperity

"We have been the recipients of the choicest bounties of heaven; we have been preserved these many years in peace and prosperity; we have grown in numbers, wealth and power as no other nation has ever grown.

"But we have forgotten God.

"We have forgotten the gracious hand which preserved us in peace and multiplied and enriched and strengthened us, and we have vainly imagined, in the deceitfulness of our hearts, that all these blessings were produced by some superior wisdom and virtue of our own.

"Intoxicated with unbroken success, we have become too self-sufficient to feel the necessity of redeeming and preserving grace, too proud to pray to the God that made us."

—Abraham Lincoln,
in his Thanksgiving
Proclamation, 1863.

On the Course of History

"They tell you this is a secular age, an age of science, of technology, of progress ... a post-Christian age.

"There can never be a 'post-Christian age' in all eternity. Christ is living in the hearts of millions who know Him and love Him. The Bible has never been distributed or read all over the world more than today. At the rate at which people are accepting Christ today in Africa, the continent below the Sahara will before the end of the century be a Christian continent for the first time in history.

"The amazing Christian ferment in the United States in all its diverse manifestations is encouraging, although it is not yet a full-fledged national revival. Jesus Christ is everywhere; He is behind everything we see if only we have eyes to see Him; and He is the Lord of history if only we penetrate deep enough beneath the surface."

—Charles Malik,
former Secretary-General,
the United Nations.

On Unity

"I am increasingly convinced that in Jesus Christ

and the community of faith, we have the power and the models to draw us together. Faith holds our world together."

—former President
Gerald Ford.

Open Door Policy

As a young girl, Fanny Crosby, the famous blind hymnwriter, often dictated poetry to the secretary of New York's Institute for the Blind. In later decades, when the man became nationally famous, his office doors were still open for Fanny Crosby if she wanted to dictate.

The man, Grover Cleveland, had moved his office to the White House as President of the United States.

Patriotic Bird

President William McKinley enjoyed the talents of a pet parrot who could complete the tune of "Yankee Doodle" once McKinley whistled the first few bars.

Peter Minuit

Peter Minuit bought Manhattan Island from the Indians in 1636 for trinkets valued at about $24. In 1638 he established an outpost at what is now Wilmington, Delaware, and called it Fort Christina in honor of the Swedish Queen. Two years later the first Lutheran minister to step on American soil arrived there and established services.

Swedish missionaries followed a half century later and built what became known as "Old Swedes Church." Today it is the oldest church in the United States still standing as originally built and regularly used for religious services.

Professional Author

Hannah Adams, said to have been the first American woman to write professionally, was born in Medfield, Massachusetts in 1755. She began writing at the age of 17 in order to support herself after her father experienced severe financial reverses. Her life was founded solidly upon Scripture. Her first compilation eventually became known as the *Dictionary of Religions*. She also wrote *A Summary History of New England* and *The Truth and Excellence of the Christian Religion*.

Secretary of Transportation

Elizabeth Dole, Secretary of Transportation and an evangelical Christian, is the first woman to serve in this high Cabinet position.

"I could not imagine taking on such a task," Dole told an audience after her appointment, "if it were not within His plan for me, for I knew it would require strength, wisdom, and courage far beyond my own."

Mrs. Dole is the wife of Senator Robert Dole of Kansas.

Sequoyah

As early as 1821, missionaries and Cherokee Chief Sequoyah, a remarkable linguist for whom California's Sequoia redwoods were named, teamed up to launch America's first Indian newspaper. Based in Georgia, the missionaries worked closely with Indian leaders and the newspaper's editor, Elias Boudinot. Boudinot, himself a product of Indian missions, later became one of the early presidents of the American Bible Society.

Tough Opponent

Peter Cartwright, one of the most famous circuit-riding preachers of the early frontier, once ran for a seat in Congress but was defeated. His opponent was Abraham Lincoln.

U. S. Doctor

America's first woman doctor, Elizabeth Blackwell, an evangelical Christian, was the daughter of a wealthy sugar merchant whose family had come to America in 1833 to escape religious persecution in England. Though admitted to Geneva College (N.Y.) Medical School as a joke, she graduated at the head of her class. Blackwell founded the nation's first medical college for women in New York City in 1857.

White House Events

President Richard Nixon hosted Sunday worship services in the White House.

President Jimmy Carter hosted a gospel sing on the White House lawn.

William McKinley

William McKinley was a devout Christian, taught a Bible class, and was superintendent of a Methodist Sunday School. He was also devoted to his mother. As a lawyer, congressman, Governor of Ohio, and, finally, President of the United States, when William McKinley did not see his mother he either wrote or telegraphed her each day of her life.

When McKinley's mother became ill in the winter of 1897, he had her home in Canton, Ohio connected with the White House by special wire and kept a special train standing by under full steam.

One night McKinley's assistants wired from Ohio: "Mr. President, we think you had better come."

McKinley flashed back his answer: "Tell Mother I'll be there."

His mother later died in the arms of her presidential son.

In Buffalo, New York, less than four years later, an assassin's bullet took the President's life.

Hymnwriter Charles Fillmore, inspired by a newspaper account of McKinley's telegram to those at his dying mother's bedside, later wrote a song, "Tell Mother I'll Be There," about the incident.

Wilson: "PK"

Woodrow Wilson was the son of a Presbyterian minister. When he was a boy, his father pastored the First Presbyterian Church of Augusta, Georgia.

Black Hills

America's most well-known passion play is performed on an outdoor stage in the Black Hills town, Spearfish, South Dakota, during the summer. (In the winter the play moves to Lake Wales, Florida.)

Josef Meier has played the lead role of Jesus since 1939. When Meier first brought the original cast to the United States from Germany, its actors struggled so with the English language that most of them returned to Europe. Meier determined to stay and conquer the language obstacle. He has now given more than 6,000 performances.

Glass Masterpiece

A 30-foot-wide mosaic of the ascension hangs at Forest Lawn Memorial Park in Glendale, California. It consists of over a million pieces of Venetian glass in 3,000 shades of color.

Jerome Hines

Jerome Hines of New York's Metropolitan Opera wrote an opera on the life of Christ titled, "I am the Way." A forthright Christian, Hines took the opera on the road and even into Russia where he received standing ovations.

Laguna Beach Arts Festival

At California's annual Laguna Beach Arts Festival, Leonardo da Vinci's painting, "The Last Supper" is portrayed by people dressed in authentic costume who hold their poses with such absence of movement that the scene appears to be a three-dimensional painting. Always the last scene of the annual show, it inevitably draws an ovation.

Largest Religious Painting

The world's largest religious painting, "The Crucifixion," by Polish-born artist Jan Styka, hangs in the Hall of the Crucifixion-Resurrection at Forest Lawn Memorial Park in Glendale, California. In a brief program that repeats every 30 minutes, narration, special lighting and dramatic sound effects effectively bring the painting "alive" to the thousands who view it each month.

Unlike other artists, who show Jesus on the cross, Styka chose to portray that moment *before* Christ was placed upon the cross of Calvary.

The painting of the Crucifixion was conceived by Poland's famous musician-statesman, Ignace Jan Paderewski, who was Styka's compatriot.

Largest Stained Glass Window

The largest stained glass window in the world is not in a church. Rather, the window is at Kennedy International Airport in New York City. The window, located in the American Airlines terminal building, measures 300-feet long by 23-feet high.

Last Supper Drama

Christus Gardens, a popular year-round tourist

attraction in Gatlinburg, Tennessee, at the base of the Smoky Mountains, dramatizes Leonardo da Vinci's famous painting of "The Last Supper" in wax figures that "come to life." Some disciples talk, some dine, and one clutches a bag of silver. Choral music backdrops the drama. The figures are lifesize, hand-crafted by master artists, and robed in garments authentic in every detail.

Moby Dick

Herman Melville's vivid descriptions of church found in chapters seven and eight of his book, *Moby Dick*, reflect his boyhood memories of Seamen's Bethel in New Bedford, Massachusetts, the church he attended on Johnny Cake Hill. Today the church has marked the pew in which Melville sat as an eight-year-old.

Melville based his novel on a real whale named Mocha Dick, who terrorized the seas in the mid-1800's. Mocha Dick caused the deaths of more than 30 men, sank five ships and survived 19 harpoons.

1984

In 1984, a passion play dramatized by 100 of evangelist Jack Wyrtzen's Word of Life Collegians aired on prime-time television.

Oberammergau

The world's most famous passion play—the drama of Jesus' last week on earth and the Crucifixion—is held in Oberammergau, Germany.

Passion Plays in America

The nation's second most popular passion play runs from May to October at Eureka Springs, Arkansas. It requires a cast of 200. Spectator seating capacity is 4,200.

Still another passion play, the Smoky Mountain Passion Play, plays each summer in Townsend, Tennessee, but alternates with a drama on the life of the Apostle Paul. It has a much smaller cast and a less elaborate, more rustic setting than the Eureka Springs Passion Play.

Pilgrim's Progress

Pilgrim's Progress, an allegory on Christian life, has been the world's best selling book, except for the Bible, over the past centuries.

Robinson Crusoe

Sailor Robinson Crusoe, in the classic book, *Robinson Crusoe*, was a born-again Christian in the original unabridged text. He also tried to lead his man Friday, a native whom he had rescued from the cannibals, to Jesus Christ. But since the book first appeared in 1841, publishers have so secularized it that the Christian content no longer remains.

Shepherd/Author

Phillip Keller, famous Canadian shepherd and Christian author, enriches his devotional books with his first-hand knowledge of sheep and their ways. His several books, including *A Shepherd Looks at the 23rd Psalm*, have ranked among evangelical bestsellers.

"The Messiah"

George Frederick Handel wrote his immortal work, "The Messiah," after he had worked and prayed almost continually for twenty-three days and nights.

Uncle Tom's Cabin

Harriet Beecher Stowe, author of *Uncle Tom's Cabin*, was the daughter of Lyman Beecher, probably the most powerful Puritan preacher of his time. Three of Harriet's brothers also became influential preachers, but her antislavery novel made the greatest impact of all on the nation.

Stowe based the character of Uncle Tom on a real slave, Josiah Henson, who was born in Maryland in 1769, escaped from Maryland to Canada, and became a Methodist preacher.

Wax Masterpiece

In Fort Worth, Texas, a life-size wax figure interpretation of Leonardo da Vinci's famous painting, "The Last Supper," is displayed at the headquarters of the Radio and Television Commission of the Southern

Baptist Convention.

Katherine Stubergh and her daughter worked 18 months to complete the exhibit, spending hundreds of hours placing human hairs in each head and beard—some 40,000 strands in each.

Wildlife Artist/Missionary

Phil Lasz combines a missionary career with wildlife art. Joy Adamson, the late author of *Born Free*, once said that Lasz is " . . . unmistakably bound for the top in wildlife art."

Lasz went on his first African safari as a small child (his missionary parents took him, but he does not remember it). On a "safari" today he takes only a camera and telephoto lens. The resulting photos help him paint animals and the surrounding terrain with authenticity of detail. Yet Lasz sees his wildlife art as only a sideline and gives half of his profits from it to the Lord's work.

Food and Hunger

FLOUR

Apples and the Gospel

The *Mayflower* Pilgrims and the Jamestown settlers brought apple seeds to America. In later years John Chapman roamed the country planting thousands of apple trees and exchanging apple seeds for food and clothing. While doing so, he also spread the gospel through the use of religious tracts. In time John Chapman became known simply as "Johnny Appleseed."

A Product is Born

Evangelical churches of the 1880's who were uncomfortable with the idea of using fermented wine in communion found another option in the product of Dr. Thomas Bremwell Welch. He offered churches Dr. Welch's Unfermented Wine. Later it was introduced to the public at the 1893 Chicago World's Fair under a new label: Welch's Grape Juice.

Famine in Africa

More than 400,000 people died in a famine that spread across central and southern Africa in 1973. Current drought conditions in this same area raise fears that the tragedy could happen again.

Food Baskets

Christian students who gathered in Kansas City during Christmas week of 1983 personally distributed bags of food to more than 1,000 needy Kansas City families. More than 1,000 other families came to pick up their own bags. This distribution included 40,000 pounds of grapefruit and 20,000 pounds of potatoes and dried beans.

Graham Cracker

Billy Graham did not invent the "Graham" cracker. Rather, it is made of graham flour which was named after Sylvester Graham, a New England minister. Graham (1794-1851), incidentally, also preached vigorously against "tea, coffee and feather beds."

Henry J. Heinz

When Henry J. Heinz chose the slogan, "57 Varieties," to describe his line of food products, he had built New York City's first large electric sign—it was six stories high and had 1,200 lights—to advertise "57 Good Things for the Table." The sign included a 40-foot pickle.

Heinz was known as a forthright Christian who was unafraid to speak of salvation and his Savior.

Natural Site

When Japanese-born Dr. Tetsunao Yamamori assumed his duties in May, 1984, as the new president of Food for the Hungry, a worldwide evangelical relief agency, his installation occurred in a most appropriate site: the traditional spot near the Sea of Galilee where the Lord Jesus Christ multiplied the loaves and fish in the "feeding of the 5,000."

Peanut Coffee?

George Washington Carver, a devout Christian who won international fame as a scientist and agriculturalist, started each day at four o'clock with a quiet time. He found more than 300 uses for the common peanut, including "coffee." He also put sweet potatoes and soybeans to many uses.

Poverty Specialist

John Perkins, founder of Voice of Calvary Ministries in Mississippi and the only black on the Presidential Task Force on Food Assistance (the President's "Hunger Commission"), has transformed thousands of lives by the gospel and his innovative approaches to poverty. In Mississippi, Perkins has pioneered efforts in organizing housing companies, health care systems, co-op ventures, and educational institutions.

Solomon the Gourmet

King Solomon had 12 officers who provided food for the king and his immense household. Each man was responsible for one month of the year (I Kings 4:7). One day's requirements for Solomon's 40,000 horses and 12,000 horsemen included 300 bushels of fine flour, 600 bushels of meal, 30 oxen, 100 sheep, plus deer and fowl with barley and straw for the animals.

Story of a Breakfast Cereal

C. W. Post introduced a breakfast cereal in 1904 called Elijah's Manna. The name drew flak from clergymen so Post gave it a new label to avoid criticism. He called the cereal Post Toasties.

Story of the Sundae

The ice-cream sundae really has something to do with Sunday. A century ago in the Midwest, many towns had laws prohibiting the sale of ice-cream sodas on Sunday. But some shop owners found a way to obey the letter of the law, if not its spirit. They simply left out the carbonated water, leaving only the ice cream and the syrup. And that is how the sundae was born.

Bethlehem, U.S.A.

Bethlehem, Pennsylvania, home of Bethlehem Steel, was founded on a cold Christmas Eve in 1741 when a small group of Moravians from Germany gathered for a hymn and prayer service. Count Zinzendorf, patron of these evangelistic pioneers, was inspired to give the town its name. It was a Boston pastor, Phillips Brooks, however, who wrote the hymn, "O Little Town of Bethlehem."

Cards of the Presidents

While in office, President Carter and the First Lady sent 60,000 Christmas cards each season. In contrast, the Eisenhowers mailed only 1,300 cards each year.

Christmas Fireworks

Christmas fireworks celebrations are common in Italy, France, Spain, and China. French settlers introduced the tradition to New Orleans.

Christmas Lights

Martin Luther was the first to use lighted candles on a Christmas tree, but the early inhabitants of New Mexico first created the "farolito" to light the way for the Christ Child on Christmas Eve. The farolito consists of votive candles, which are set in the center of paper sacks half-filled with sand and used to line streets and drives on Christmas Eve. This traditional lighting may still be seen in New Mexico today.

Christmas Seals

Einar Holboll, a Danish postmaster, is given credit for the Christmas seal idea. He saw it as a means of raising money for a worthy cause and issued the first Christmas seals in Denmark in 1904. By the time of his death two decades later, his idea had caught hold in countries around the world.

The U. S. uses the Christmas seal primarily to fight tuberculosis, but the American Bible Society also issues seals at Christmas time to fund translation and distribution of the Bible throughout the world.

Christmas Stamps

For several years the United States Post Office has issued two Christmas stamps each season—one with a religious, one with a secular theme.

Christmas Tree Lights

Martin Luther is credited with the idea of putting lights on a Christmas tree. According to legend, he got his inspiration while walking home one Christmas Eve. At one point he glanced up, says the story, and saw stars shining through the snow-covered branches of a fir tree. In an attempt later to describe the beautiful scene to his family, he placed some lighted candles on the branches of his own Christmas tree. From that time on, says the legend, it became a Luther family tradition.

107

Community Christmas Tree

Parisians lit the first "community" Christmas tree. In 1909, the citizens of Pasadena, California, illuminated a tall evergreen atop nearby Mt. Wilson. New York and Boston first lit public trees in 1912, Philadelphia in 1914.

Cypress Gardens

The "Radio Bible Class" of Grand Rapids, Michigan, conducts one of the nation's most popular televised Easter sunrise services each year in beautiful Cypress Gardens in central Florida.

Death Valley

Easter sunrise services are held each year in Death Valley, California, one of the world's hottest spots. Death Valley, 282 feet below sea level, is also the lowest point in the United States.

Easter Lilies

A Philadelphia nurseryman brought the first Easter lily bulbs to the U. S. from Bermuda in the 1880's.

Lincoln's Initiative

President Abraham Lincoln designated the first official Thanksgiving Day in 1863. Until that time it had been celebrated only by the people of New England.

Marion, Indiana Spectacle

Each Easter morning in Marion, Indiana, the town's coliseum turns into the streets of Jerusalem. More than 2,000 people, including 500 in makeup and costume, stage the annual Marion Easter Pageant. The performance includes a 500-voice chorus and a 100-piece orchestra.

During the dramatic one-hour pageant, the actors speak no words. In pantomime, pageantry, and music alone, they dramatize the last week of Christ's life on earth.

At the pageant conclusion no credits are given—not even for the man who plays the role of Jesus Christ—no salaries paid, no admission charged. It is entirely the work of volunteers.

Mother's Day

At a church in Grafton, West Virginia, in May, 1905, Ann M. Jarvis arranged a special service in memory of her mother who had recently died. The idea of a tribute to mothers caught on. By 1914 the United States officially recognized Mother's Day.

Norwegian Candles

Norwegians install three candles on the tops of their Christmas trees. The candles represent the three Wise Men.

Origin of the Christmas Wreath

The Christmas wreath has its origins in the Crown

of Thorns placed upon the head of Christ before His crucifixion.

Thanksgiving Square

A triangular block in downtown Dallas, Texas has been set aside as "Thanks-Giving Square." Bordered by Pacific, Ervay and Bryan, the square includes waterfalls, carpet, bronze bells on a fifty-foot tower, and a "Chapel of Thanks-Giving."

The First Christmas Cards

Louis Prang, a German immigrant in Boston, produced the first American Christian Christmas cards in about 1875. They were of exceptional quality.

The Pilgrims' Menu

The menu of the first Pilgrim Thanksgiving is supposed to have included venison steak cooked over an outdoor fire; spit-roasted wild turkeys stuffed with corn bread; oysters baked in their shells; sweet corn baked in its husks; and pumpkin baked in a bag and flavored with maple syrup.

The President Forgets

In 1865, Thanksgiving Day was celebrated on December 7. That year President Andrew Johnson had forgotten to proclaim the third Thursday of November as the day of the event.

Yellowstone's Christmas in August

Each year Yellowstone National Park celebrates Christmas in August. The idea originated years ago when collegians serving under "A Christian Ministry in National Parks," decided to inspire park visitors with a performance of the "Messiah." The celebration has now become a tradition.

A Gift for Moody

The A. C. Nielsen Co. of Chicago, which measures audience response to the nation's television shows, in 1976 gave the building which for many years had housed its national headquarters, to the Moody Bible Institute.

The building now accommodates the operations of Moody Press, *Moody Monthly Magazine* and the Moody Correspondence School.

A Printer of Conviction

Hart Press, a large magazine publishing plant in rurally located Long Prairie, Minnesota, prints more of the nation's evangelical magazines than any other single contract printer. Among them are the Wheaton-based magazines *Christianity Today, Partnership, Leadership, Campus Life, Christian Reader, Venture, Dash* and *Trails*, as well as the two magazines which are published by Back to the Bible Broadcast in Lincoln, Nebraska.

Although Hart Press also prints numerous secular magazines, it flatly refuses any magazine of a pornographic nature. In so doing it has turned down millions of dollars in potential business.

A Rumor That Will Not Die

Since a 1975 legal issue in Los Angeles, more than 15.5 million letters—at the rate of 135,000 a month—have flooded the Federal Communications Commission (FCC) protesting an alleged petition by Madalyn Murray O'Hair to remove religious programming from the air.

Despite the rumors and the incredible volume of mail, no such petition ever existed.

In 1979, *Washington Insight*, a monthly newsletter of the National Association of Evangelicals, theorized that "enemies of Christianity might be keeping the rumor alive to make Christians look foolish." These suspicions were confirmed in October, 1983, by Mrs. O'Hair's son, William J. Murray, now a Christian.

"Part of [Murray's] responsibility, when a vice-president of the American Atheist Center," reported *Washington Insight*, "was to keep the fake petitions in circulation."

Al Hartley/"Archie"

Al Hartley, son of the co-author of the Taft-Hartley Act, turned his life over to the Lord after friends invited him to a prayer meeting. Shortly afterward, his editor asked Hartley to take over the drawing of "Archie Comics," which already appeared in over 850 newspapers around the world.

"It was an unbelievable opportunity," Hartley says. Though proceeding cautiously with his superiors, Hartley eventually made Archie, a lovable freckle-faced teenager, into a born-again Christian.

The story of this transformation is told in the comic book, "Archie's Clean Slate," sold in many Christian bookstores. Over 60 million comic books featuring Archie and his friends are sold yearly.

Brazil

Brazil will soon have a Christian television station

that will reach 40 million people and that will have the potential to expand its signal to cover the entire nation which encompasses about half of the South American continent. Brazil's President granted a TV broadcasting license worth $1.5 million to a production company formed by the pastor of Brazil's largest Baptist church in Rio de Janeiro to operate the station.

Charles Schultz/"Peanuts"

Charles Schultz, creator of "Peanuts," considered by many as the world's most popular comic strip, was graduated from Anderson College, an evangelical Christian school, in Anderson, Indiana. The school has displayed some of Schultz's original cartoon strips in its hallways in recognition of its famous alumnus.

At the time he launched "Peanuts," Schultz was a cartoonist for the St. Paul (Minnesota) *Pioneer Press*.

Occasionally, Schultz injects theological meaning into his cartoon story line.

Christian Radio Grows

There are now more than 1,000 religious radio stations in the United States. Many are licensed as noncommercial stations; some are commercial.

Christian Television

Ten years ago the United States had no Christian television stations. Today it has more than 80, reports the National Association of Religious Broadcasters.

Christian television programs do not keep people from attending church according to a 1984 survey conducted by the University of Pennsylvania's Annenberg School of Communications.

In fact, evidence even suggests that Christian television contributes to the growth of the church. Some 13.3 million people regularly watch religious programs, about 6.2 percent of the estimated number of people in households with televisions.

Christian TV for Teens

Christian teenagers in Kansas City run their own television station. The station, KYFC-TV, is owned by Youth for Christ. It was purchased by YFC in 1979 for $2.5 million.

Exchange

When pornography publisher Larry Flynt sent free subscriptions of *Hustler* magazine to all members of the U.S. Senate, Senator Charles Grassley (R-Iowa), an evangelical, sent Flynt a gift subscription to *Christianity Today*.

First Chorale

In 1946 the Moody Chorale of Chicago was the first college-related choral group in the nation to adopt the term "chorale" as a part of its name.

Radio

The Moody Broadcasting Network, now with more than 70 affiliate stations, is the largest and fastest-growing Christian radio system in the nation. Within a few years it expects to have more than 500 affiliate stations.

The expansion has been made possible, in part, by America's satellite technology by which the Moody radio signal is bounced to almost any part of North America from 22,300 miles above the earth.

Radio Drama Still Lives

"Unshackled," a popular drama program heard on more than 500 stations worldwide, is the nation's oldest radio drama. The 30-minute program, produced by the Pacific Garden Mission in Chicago, dramatizes the conversion stories of those who have found the answer to life in Jesus Christ.

Reagan and the Religious Broadcasters

President Reagan's first public appearance after he had declared his candidacy for a second term was at the National Religious Broadcasters meeting in Washington, D.C. Said the Chief Executive, "If we could get God and discipline back in our schools, maybe we could get drugs and violence out."

Shortwave Superpowers

Superpower shortwave Christian stations of Trans-World Radio, the Far Eastern Broadcasting Company, and World Radio Missionary Fellowship send the gospel into all parts of the world including Communist lands where missionaries cannot go.

Station KGEI, its antenna situated south of San Francisco, beams the gospel directly over the North Pole into Soviet Russia.

Shortwave radio travels great distances because these waves bounce off the ionosphere. Dr. Louis Muggleton, a physicist, mapped the entire ionosphere and has concluded that its only function is the reflection of radio waves. Some have suggested that God constructed these reflecting layers at the time of creation as part of His strategy for world evangelism in the 20th century.

Superpower in Chicago

WCFL-AM/Chicago, long rated as one of the nation's more powerful stations, introduced a Christian music and talk-show format in May, 1984. A Florida Christian group purchased the station from the Mutual Broadcasting Network for $8 million. The signal of WCFL-AM, originally owned by the Chicago Federation of Labor, for which its call letters stand, can be heard at night in as many as 24 states.

On Chicago's FM scene, Moody Bible Institute's Radio WMBI has long ranked as the city's evangelical voice.

The World Listens In

In 1979 the world's people owned over one billion radio sets, one for every four people on earth.

Unusual Hobby

Claude Chilton, a former pastor and U. S. Air Force chaplain, decided to see how many different religious magazines he could collect in his retirement. At last count he had 9,250 magazines. His collection includes: *Christian Railroad, Voice of the Christian Trucker,* and *Humorneutics*.

Wayne Stayskal/Chicago *Tribune*

Wayne Stayskal, editorial cartoonist of the *Chicago Tribune*, has been syndicated nationally since 1962. His associates know him as a committed evangelical Christian. So, also, was Stayskal's *Tribune* predecessor, the late Vaughan Shoemaker, who received the Pulitzer Prize.

World Christian TV Network

The Southern Baptist Radio and Television Commission is attempting to assemble the world's largest Christian TV network. Its programs are expected to air on approximately 1,000 cable systems and reach 40 million people.

World Network

The evangelical Far Eastern Broadcasting Company has a network of 28 short- and medium-wave radio stations around the globe. Their combined 1.5 million watts of power broadcast 270 program hours per day in more than 90 languages.

A Flag in the Night

The flag over Fort McHenry, at Baltimore, Maryland, remains at full mast around the clock by Presidential law. When the long bombardment that inspired Francis Scott Key to pen "The Star-Spangled Banner" had finally ceased, the original Fort McHenry flag had 11 holes in it.

Amy's Record

At age 23, singer Amy Grant became the first gospel artist to receive a gold album from the Recording Industry Association of America. Sales of her 1982 album, *Age To Age*, surpassed one-half million. She has captured three Dove Awards and two Grammies. In an article called "Amy's World," *Life* magazine (November, 1984) gave her five pages of coverage. Said Amy in *Life*: "I just want to make it very clear that I'm going to continue to sing about the Lord. That's where my heart is. I want my audiences to find what I have found."

"All Creatures of Our God and King"

"All Creatures of Our God and King" is more than 750 years old. It was written by St. Francis of Assisi in 1225, a year before his death.

Also a Poet

While most Americans know that Francis Scott Key

wrote "The Star-Spangled Banner," most are unaware that he also wrote Christian poetry. One of his poems, "Lord, With Glowing Heart I'd Praise Thee," still appears in some hymnals.

Away in a Manger

Many have long credited Martin Luther with the Christmas hymn, "Away in a Manger" (often called "Luther's Cradle Hymn"). But more recent evidence suggests the hymn originated not with Luther in Germany, but with the German Lutherans of early Pennsylvania.

Bargain Sale

In the late 1940's, while a student at Chicago's Moody Bible Institute, songwriter John Peterson sold ten songs for $40 to radio evangelist Percy Crawford. One of the songs, "It Took a Miracle," became known worldwide and was eventually recorded by well-known performers like Kate Smith and Eddie Arnold.

As a World War II pilot, Peterson flew 100 missions over the Himalayas, the world's tallest mountains, where the majesty of God and His protection were embedded in Peterson's experience.

Bob Jones University

Bob Jones University in Greenville, South Carolina

stages two operas annually. Often, one is in a lighter vein and uses university talent exclusively, while the other, a grand opera, engages the leading singers of the world to appear with the University Opera Association chorus and orchestra.

Charles Wesley

Charles Wesley, brother of John Wesley and author of some 6,500 hymns, was once secretary to Governor Oglethorpe, founder of Georgia.

Choral Notes

The Christian choral group long known as the "Sixteen Singing Men" has usually recorded with one woman singing with the men.

Christian Concerts at Amusement Parks

Christian concerts have become annual events at several prominent Southern California amusement parks. It started ten years ago with a trial concert at Disneyland in which gospel groups mixed with crowds totaling 20,000 sending the strains of "Alleluia" from Disneyland's front gate along its Main Street.

Knott's Berry Farm sponsors an annual fall concert night called "Jubilation," and also a "Christian New Year's Eve" party. In June, Six Flags Magic Mountain holds a "Hallelujah Jubilee." Christian groups have also appeared at Sea World and Marineland.

Flag Carrier

Fanny Crosby, blind hymnwriter, always carried a small American flag with her. She either held it in her hand or kept it in her purse. It was buried with her when she died in 1915 at the age of 95.

"God Bless America"

Songwriter Irving Berlin's "God Bless America" was first sung on radio in 1938 by Kate Smith. The song won Berlin the Congressional Gold Medal. He gave the royalties the song earned to the Girl Scouts and Boy Scouts of America.

Gospel Market

The gospel market accounted for nearly six percent of last year's $3.8 billion sales of records and tapes. Gospel music now outsells both jazz and classical.

"Hark! The Herald Angels Sing"

Charles Wesley, brother of John Wesley, founder of Methodism, wrote the words to "Hark! The Herald Angels Sing," but the melody was adapted from the music of Mendelssohn.

Hymn Notes

The music of Henry Van Dyke's "Joyful, Joyful We Adore Thee" is adapted from Beethoven's "Ninth Symphony."

Hymn of the "Titanic"

In April 1912, when the luxury liner "Titanic" sank in the icy waters of the north Atlantic, the ship's band reportedly was playing the hymn, "Nearer My God to Thee." Many of the 1500 passengers still aboard the ship when its few lifeboats had been filled were singing the hymn, according to the story.

"I Heard the Bells on Christmas Day"

Poet Henry Wadsworth Longfellow wrote the words to "I Heard the Bells on Christmas Day."

Jeremiah Rankin

Jeremiah Rankin, who wrote the words to "God Be With You 'Til We Meet Again," was for 13 years president of Washington's Howard University, which was founded in 1867 for the higher education of Negroes.

Joseph Gilmore

Joseph Gilmore, who authored the words of the hymn, "He Leadeth Me," was the son of a New Hampshire governor.

"Joy to the World"

The music for "Joy to the World" was adapted by Lowell Mason from a portion of Handel's "Messiah." Hymnwriter Isaac Watts wrote the words in 1719.

Lake Chautauqua

Lake Chautauqua, in the Finger Lakes region of western New York, helped inspire the hymn, "Break Thou the Bread of Life." Mary A. Lathbury, talented artist and writer of the early-day "Chautauqua movement" wrote the hymn in 1877 after meditating by the lakeside during a summer conference and envisioning Christ feeding the five thousand on the hillside by Galilee.

Lake Erie Shipwreck

Evangelist Dwight L. Moody gave Philip P. Bliss the idea for his hymn, "Let the Lower Lights Be Burning," when Bliss heard Moody tell the true story of a ship that had crashed onto the rocks of Lake Erie near Cleveland. The ship's passengers were lost because the lower lights along the shore were out.

Only the main light of the lighthouse itself was burning.

Lake Michigan

In 1911 William Person Merrill wrote the hymn, "Rise Up, O Men of God," while taking a Lake Michigan steamer to Chicago.

Lake Ontario Inspiration

Lake Ontario, in part, inspired the hymn, "This is My Father's World." As a young pastor in Lockport, New York, Maltbie Babcock often said to his congregation, "I am going out to see my Father's world." Whereupon he would run to the summit of a hill about two miles outside the city and enjoy the sounds of a bird sanctuary together with a view of the surrounding terrain and the panorama of nearby Lake Ontario.

Milestone

Gospel soloist George Beverly Shea, who still sings in Billy Graham crusades, celebrated his 75th birthday in March, 1984.

Most Popular Hymn

"The Old Rugged Cross" has become one of the most popular hymns of all time. The Rev. George

Bennard started writing the hymn in 1912 and first sang the completed version, with his guitar, in his parsonage kitchen on the corner of College Court and Michigan Avenue in Albion, Michigan. The home has since been torn down, but today a plaque stands on the site.

In 1953 Bennard was invited to ride in the Pasadena Rose Parade aboard "The Old Rugged Cross" float. There, on a flower-covered organ, he played his famous song for the largest live audience of his lifetime.

Most Prolific Hymnwriter

Fanny Crosby (1820-1915) wrote more than 8,000 hymns in her lifetime—even though she was blind. Among her best known are "To God Be the Glory" and "Jesus is Calling." Her personal favorite was "Safe in the Arms of Jesus."

Musician on the Spot

Ira Sankey composed the music to "The Ninety and Nine," based on the parable of the lost sheep, before a live audience.

Evangelist Dwight L. Moody had just delivered a message on "The Good Shepherd" to a large crowd, and Sankey, caught by surprise, found himself unprepared for an appropriate closing solo. Earlier in the week Sankey had clipped a poem titled, "The Ninety and Nine," from a local newspaper while he and Moody traveled by train.

Sankey, deciding to use the poem, composed the music and the vocal solo as he went along. The hymn was an instant success and remained almost exactly as it had been sung that night when, in desperation, Sankey had decided to "wing it."

National Gospel Quartet Convention

A National Gospel Quartet Convention is held the second week in October in Nashville.

Navy Hymn

The United States Navy has adopted "Eternal Father, Strong to Save" as its official hymn and the school hymn of the U. S. Naval Academy in Annapolis. A beautiful French translation has also made the hymn a standard part of the hymn book of the French Navy.

The hymn's prayer not only calls for protection at sea but also in the air and on land.

Old Hymns

The hymn, "Jesus, Thou Joy of Loving Hearts," more than 800 years old, is believed to have been written by Bernard of Clairvaux, a gifted French monk and Christian mystic who died in 1153.

Pike's Peak Inspiration

The hymn, "America the Beautiful," was penned atop Pike's Peak by Julia Ward Howe, a schoolteacher, who rode up the 14,110-foot mountain one day in a "prairie wagon." Her hymn speaks of God's blessings upon the land but also prays that America's liberties will not be abused. "Confirm thy soul in self-control," she writes, and "liberty in law."

President/Hymnwriter

President John Quincy Adams, who served as an early president of the American Bible Society, wrote "Poems of Religion and Society" and also Christian hymns including "Sure to the Mansions of the Blest" (1803) and "Alas! How Swift the Moments Fly" (1839).

Sea Convert

John Newton, who authored "Amazing Grace" in 1779, had sailed the high seas as a debauched slave trader before he was converted as he read Thomas a Kempis' book, *Imitation of Christ*, during a long voyage from Brazil.

The hymn he later wrote testified, in his own words, to the tremendous grace of God.

In later years Newton pastored a little church in Olney, England, but he never gave up his sea garb. Newton walked the pulpit dressed like a sailor—with a cane in one hand and a Bible in the other.

Sea Pulpit

Edward Hopper, who wrote the words of "Jesus, Savior, Pilot Me" in 1871, pastored the Church of the Sea and Land on the shores of New York harbor.

Small Sale

Julia Ward Howe sold "The Battle Hymn of the Republic" to the *Atlantic Monthly* magazine in 1861 for only $5.00.

"The First Noel"

Some authorities believe "The First Noel" has early English beginnings and that "Nowell" is a contraction of the phrase, "Now all is well."

The National Anthem

Francis Scott Key wrote "The Star-Spangled Banner" while an overnight prisoner on a British ship in Chesapeake Bay in August 1814. At one time Key had debated whether he wanted to be a lawyer or a minister. His choice of law, and his success in it, gave him the expertise to negotiate with the British on that historic night during the War of 1812 when he watched "the bombs bursting in air." Yet, his evangelical faith gave him the wisdom to call for a nation that would put its trust in God.

After the war, "The Star-Spangled Banner" caught on quickly in Baltimore, but did not become nationally known until half a century later—after the Civil War. And, it did not become America's official national anthem until 1931 during the administration of Herbert Hoover.

The Sounds of Music

At Estes Park, the Rocky Mountains come alive with the sound of Christian music early every August. The Colorado village is the site of the annual "Music Seminar in the Rockies," a serious week-long smorgasbord of workshops for hundreds of youth and adult musicians. Workshops include gospel song-writing, graded choir programs, vocal techniques, multimedia, choreography, instrumental classes, piano, songleading, and television production. Evening concerts, packed with the talent of Christian artists, are open to the public.

Top Concerts

Wheaton (Illinois) College, one of the oldest and most prominent of evangelical colleges in America, has hosted on its campus such outstanding artists as the Robert Shaw Chorale, Isaac Stern, and the Boston Symphony Orchestra.

Where "America" Went Public

A Baptist minister, Dr. Samuel Francis Smith, wrote the hymn, "America" ("My Country, 'Tis of Thee") in 1831. It took Dr. Smith half an hour to scrawl the song on a sheet of paper. It was first sung the same year at the Park Street Church in Boston, located at the head of Boston's historic "Freedom Trail."

Winona Sunset

One evening in 1936 a colorful sunset over Winona Lake, Indiana, site of an historic evangelical conference grounds, inspired Virgil and Blanche Brock to write the hymn, "Beyond the Sunset."

The Brocks were visiting at the time in the home of gospel music publisher Homer Rodeheaver on the lake's Rainbow Point when a blind guest in their midst commented, "I never saw a more beautiful sunset."

When Virgil Brock asked the blind man about his seemingly paradoxical remark, the man replied, "I do see through the eyes of others. I even see beyond the sunset."

The Brocks immediately went to a nearby piano and wrote the song.

"Yankee Doodle"

Until it was replaced by "The Star-Spangled Banner" in 1931, "Yankee Doodle" was the official national anthem. It was also the first tune recorded on a record.

Africa

Africa was a totally pagan continent in the mid-1800's when missionary David Livingstone explored its interior. Today it is more than half Christian.

The United States would fit into the continent of Africa three-and-a-half times.

Asheville's "Retreat" Empire

The largest U. S. retreat centers of the Methodists, the Presbyterians, and the Southern Baptists all lie within 25 miles of Asheville, North Carolina at Lake Junaluska, Montreat, and Ridgecrest. All three denominations prospered in the early pioneer religious climate of North Carolina. Thus, all three eventually located their impressive U. S. summer conference sites in this beautiful mountain setting.

Brazil Church Growth

The annual growth of the church in Brazil is 11.3 percent: that means the church doubles in seven years.

Camps and Conferences

Some one million Americans each year attend one of the nation's more than 700 Christian camps and conferences, according to the Christian Camps and

Conference Association. One hundred of these camps are in California. There are none in Vermont.

Camps for the Blind

National Camps for Blind Children has outdoor sites across the nation for the visually impaired. The program is free to all legally blind persons. Headquarters for the group are in Lincoln, Nebraska.

Christian Airline Pilots

Several hundred airline pilots, flight attendants, and aircraft mechanics now comprise the growing Fellowship of Christian Airline Personnel (FCAP). The movement holds a retreat each year either at Covenant College, atop Lookout Mountain near Chattanooga, Tennessee, or at Glen Eyrie, national headquarters of The Navigators near Colorado Springs, Colorado.

A Delta Airlines pilot in Atlanta and a United Airlines pilot in Chicago conceived the idea of the movement, almost simultaneously, more than a decade ago.

Christian Nurses

Nearly two thousand nurses and nursing students are active in chapters of the Nurse's Christian

Fellowship (NCF), an arm of the campus-oriented Inter-Varsity Christian Fellowship. The new NCF quarterly magazine, *Journal of Christian Nursing*, premiered in the spring of 1984.

Daisy Dell

On Easter dawn in 1921, several thousand people gathered for religious services on a Hollywood hillside known as "Daisy Dell." It was the first public event on the site, and even the Los Angeles Philharmonic Orchestra took part.

As the worshipers assembled, the songleader looked out over the weeds and grass and commented on the good acoustics because the site was shaped like a "huge bowl." The remark stuck, and soon everyone referred to Daisy Dell as the Hollywood Bowl.

Guatemala

Guatemala has Central America's largest evangelical populace, estimated at 20 percent or more.

Rios Montt, toppled from power in 1983 as Guatemala's president, was a Sunday School teacher who also preached weekly TV sermons to Guatemala's population of 7.2 million and vowed an end to centuries-old corruption and violence. In the process, he managed to antagonize the entrenched military and church establishment thus causing his ouster.

Homeless People

More than one million homeless people roam the streets of Calcutta, India.

Jungle Pilots in the U. S.

At least three United States sites accommodate those who fly, or are learning to fly, as missionary pilots in remote areas of the world. Waxhaw, North Carolina is the stateside base for pilots of the Jungle Aviation And Radio Service (JAARS), an arm of the Wycliffe Bible Translators. Mission Aviation Fellowship (MAF), the world's other major agency serving the mission fields of the world, has its headquarters at Redlands Airport in southern California. Moody Bible Institute of Chicago, which has trained half of the world's missionary pilots, headquarters its missionary aviation training program in Elizabethton, Tennessee at the edge of the Smoky Mountains.

Korean Christians

In South Korea, "Land of the Morning Calm" and home of the world's largest church congregation, more than a million evangelical Christians meet each day at dawn to pray. Many churches also have all-night Friday prayer meetings.

South Korea had 5,000 churches in 1960. Today there are 25,000. The church plants six new churches daily. Many churches also have individual home cell groups.

An estimated 45 percent of the South Korean army's 600,000 members are evangelical Christians.

Nearly 80 members of South Korea's 275-member National Assembly, the elected legislative body of the Republic, meet weekly for prayer and Bible study.

In South Korea, a gospel team can go into any high school and conduct an evangelical assembly for the entire student body during school hours.

Largest Church Congregation

The largest church congregation in the world is located in Seoul, Korea. It has a membership of more than one-quarter million. By contrast, the largest church in the United States, First Baptist Church of Dallas, Texas, has about 25,000 members.

Nicaragua

In spite of political unrest, evangelical leaders predict an evangelistic explosion in Nicaragua. Nicaragua '84, an evangelistic crusade held in the baseball stadium of Central American University in Managua, reported 36,000 decisions for Christ during a seven-day crusade early in 1984. Overflow crowds numbering as high as 80,000 on the final day taxed the capacities of the stadium.

Organizers had to shift to the stadium at the last minute when, four days before the crusade's opening, a permit to hold the crusade in the Plaza de Toros (bullfighters arena) was cancelled. Total attendance at the crusade reached 288,000.

Pedal Across America

Each year a group of Christian bicyclists, the "Wandering Wheels," bike 3,000 miles across the nation. They start the trek with their rear wheels in the Pacific Ocean and end it with their front wheels in the Atlantic.

Traveling in groups of six, they average 100 miles a day. These bikers establish habits of physical and spiritual discipline, do without the luxuries of life, and share Jesus with those along the way. They sometimes receive the key to a city and have sung to two U. S. Presidents: Harry Truman and Lyndon Johnson.

"Wandering Wheels," headquartered at Taylor University in Upland, Indiana, was founded by Bob Davenport, former All-American at UCLA, who still directs the program.

Run Across America

In 1971 brothers Tony and Joel Ahlstrom, students at Trinity College in Deerfield, Illinois, ran from Los Angeles to New York. They did so to promote ecological causes and to share the gospel.

In 1976 they ran from the Golden Gate Bridge to the White House, averaging 52 miles a day. They carried a Bible and copies of the Declaration of Independence with thousands of signatures of Americans they met along the way to President Ford.

Today Tony Ahlstrom is a chaplain to the Chicago City Council.

Runner on the Wall

In March, 1984, Stan Cottrell, a 40-year-old member of Atlanta's First Baptist Church was making plans to run 2,800 of the 4,000 miles of the Great Wall of China. He is the first person to attempt the run. As head of the Friendship Sports Association, he hopes to hold evangelistic rallies wherever the Chinese government will allow them along the Wall.

Singapore

In Singapore, second most densely populated nation in the world, nearly 24 percent of the teachers and 35.9 percent of the college-level students are Christians. Singapore's 2.4 million people live within a 226-square-mile area.

Steamtown, U. S. A.

Steamtown, U. S. A., a railroad museum and exhibit near Bellows Falls, Vermont, was founded by seafood industrialist Nelson Blount, who found Jesus Christ as his Savior after his business achievements and expensive hobbies failed to satisfy his soul. At

Steamtown, U. S. A. is the Union Pacific's "Big Boy," the largest steam locomotive ever built. The museum also offers a 22-mile excursion through the forests on the Green Mountain railroad.

The Church That Refused to Die

Communists forced missionaries from the mainland of China in 1949, closed its churches, and outlawed religion. At that time China's Christian population was estimated at about 500,000.

For more than a quarter of a century China was closed to the outside world. Some observers speculated that the Christian church in Red China had all but disappeared. But when the doors began to open again in the past decade, the Christian world was startled to learn that Christians in China now probably number in the tens of millions.

Although some churches are open again, the majority of the Christian believers meet secretly in house churches.

Trucking for Jesus

Cross-country truckers have their own movements to spread the gospel. The largest may be Transport for Christ, headquartered in Ontario, Canada. Sleek 18-wheeler mobile chapels now cruise Canadian highways, taking the church on the road and into the nation's major truck terminals. Truck chaplains show safety films and at the same time share the gospel.

Walk Across America

In the mid-1970's young rebel Peter Gorton Jenkins set out to walk the backroads of America and give it "one last chance." In Mobile, Alabama, he attended an evangelistic crusade and was converted to Jesus Christ.

When the *National Geographic* (April 1977) carried his story, "Walk Across America," it drew the largest volume of positive mail ever generated by a *National Geographic* article. Jenkins' book by the same name became a best-seller as did its sequel, *The Walk West*.

Today Jenkins and his wife, whom he met in New Orleans and who joined him in his walk west to the Oregon coastline, are raising a Christian family in Slidell, Louisiana.

World Land Speed Record

On December 17, 1979, Stan Barrett streaked down the space shuttle runway at California's Edwards Air Force Base in the Mojave Desert in a 60,000 horsepower rocket car and became the first man ever to break the sound barrier on land at a speed of 739 miles per hour.

But the most important decision he ever made, says Barrett, was the day he accepted Jesus Christ into his life, "thus breaking the barrier that existed between myself and God."

Scientific Factors

A Spherical Earth

The Greeks were the first to suggest a round earth. The Romans denied it and drew the earth as a round flat disk.

Yet centuries before the Greeks, the book of Job (oldest book in the Bible), suggested a round earth. So also did Isaiah, who refers to "the circle of the earth" (Isaiah 40:22).

In Luke 17, the words of Jesus seem to imply a round earth when He refers to His second coming, using both the phrase "in that day" (v. 31) and "in that night" (v. 34) to describe an instantaneous appearance. The passage implies the simultaneous existence of darkness and light—light on one side of the globe, darkness on the other.

A Younger Earth?

Many curious artifacts have been discovered embedded in solid rock that evolutionists say should be millions of years old. Among some of the artifacts: an eight-carat gold chain, a spoon, a thimble, an iron pot. The conclusion is that the rocks are not as old as evolutionists think.

Ancient Olive Trees

Eight olive trees estimated to be some 3,000 years old still stand in the Garden of Gethsemane where Jesus prayed and sweat drops of blood just before His Crucifixion.

Some observers say the trees are so gnarled and twisted that they seem to reflect Jesus' agony as he fell with his face to the ground and prayed, "My Father, if it be possible, let this cup pass from me...."

Average Life Expectancy

In Psalm 90:10 the Bible states that man can expect to live 70 years with some enjoying life to 80 or beyond. In 1961 the average life expectancy in the United States was 70 and has climbed only a little way beyond that in the last 20 years. Those born in 1981 may look forward to an average life expectancy of 74.1 years.

Brush Fires

Gigantic brush fires which rimmed California's San Bernardino Mountains in the fall of 1980 skipped through the grounds of Campus Crusade's international headquarters at Arrowhead Springs. While the fire did some $1 million damage to property, most of the buildings in the complex, including the organization's historic resort hotel, escaped unharmed.

On more than one occasion, similar brush fires have also threatened the campus of Westmont College in Santa Barbara.

China

The worst known earthquake in history killed 830,000 people in the Shensi Province of China in 1556. In 1976 an earthquake in China's Tangshan province killed an estimated 250,000 people.

D. L. Moody Fire

Evangelist Dwight L. Moody lost both his home and his church in the great Chicago fire of 1861. He and his wife hastily gathered up a few belongings from their home as they prepared to flee. When Mrs. Moody tried to persuade her husband to rescue a valuable painting of himself by American portrait artist G. P. A. Healy, Moody balked.

"Take my own picture!" he laughed. "That would be a joke. Suppose I meet some friends in the same trouble as ourselves and they say, 'Hullo, Moody, glad you have escaped. What's that you've saved and cling to so affectionately?'

"Wouldn't it sound well to reply, 'Oh, I've got my own portrait!' "

Looters already on the scene cut the canvas painting from its frame and handed it to Moody's wife.

Darwin's Complaint

Charles Darwin declared it a travesty that the schools of his day taught only "one view of origins": creation. Many evangelicals today agree whole-heartedly with Charles Darwin. Most schools today still teach only one view: evolution.

Earth Hanging in Space

For centuries people assumed that the earth was the fixed center of the solar system. Polish astronomer Nicolaus Copernicus challenged that assumption in 1543 when he published his theory on the motion of planetary bodies and rotation of the earth.

Sir Isaac Newton, in the next century, proposed his laws of gravitation and established firmly that the earth does indeed hang in space, held there by the gravitational forces of the sun.

Yet the book of Job, written centuries before the birth of Christ, had said so all along: "He stretches out the north over empty space, and hangs the earth on nothing" (Job 26:7, NABS).

Earthquakes

The Bible says that earthquakes will increase in "the latter days." More earthquakes have been reported in the past century than in any previous year, but some seismologists attribute this to the existence of a better earthquake reporting system today.

Evolution and Revolution

Marxism and the many modern schools of socialism were all influenced by evolutionists. Marx was so moved by Charles Darwin's theories as they applied to social order that he desired to dedicate his 1867 edition of *Das Kapital* to Charles Darwin but was refused.

First Tree Honors Corrie

Outside Jerusalem's Yad Vashem memorial, which remembers the tragic Nazi Holocaust against Jews during World War II, stand hundreds of trees, each one planted in honor of an individual who stood courageously against the anti-Semitic events of that time or who suffered in them. The "number one" tree honors the late Corrie ten Boom, a Dutch born evangelical Christian who concealed Jewish people in her father's clock shop in Holland until she and her family were finally captured and imprisoned with the Jews. Her story is vividly told in the book and the film called "The Hiding Place."

Global Seas, Four Oceans

Water covers approximately 71 percent of the earth's surface. The waters are distributed into the Atlantic, Pacific, Indian and Arctic Oceans.

Genesis 1:9 seems to describe both the "world body of water" and its individual oceans. "And God said, Let the waters under the heaven be gathered together unto one place ... " (see v. 9). Yet God also called the gathering of the waters "seas" (see v. 10), seemingly a reference to the division of the earth's waters into individual oceans.

Heavy Breather

An average tree can transpire 4,000 to 5,000 gallons of water vapor each year.

In Missouri? Show Me

The most widespread earthquake to hit the United States in modern history occurred not in the West but in the Midwest. A great earthquake on the New Madrid fault in southeast Missouri in 1803 was felt throughout the eastern United States and hit with such impact that it changed the course of the

Mississippi River.

Jamaican Farewell

In the late 1600's Port Royal, Jamaica, a wealthy town built upon the fortunes of piracy, was described by one English clergyman as "the Sodom of the New World—since the majority of its population consists of pirates, cutthroats, whores and some of the vilest persons in the whole of the world . . . . " Port Royal's Anglican pastor had once predicted that, because of its lifestyle, the town "could not stand but would sink and be destroyed by the judgment of God."

On June 7, 1692, a day hot and clear, the ground under Port Royal suddenly began to roll and heave. Multitudes of people, in only moments, were swallowed by cracks in the ground. Buildings collapsed. Within those few minutes, 1,800 homes had disappeared altogether, and the rest in the town were wrecked beyond repair.

Ocean waves rolled in upon the city. Two thousand people died immediately, and ultimately the toll rose much higher. When the earthquake had ended, all but ten acres of Port Royal had sunk into the sea.

Jerusalem

The Bible says that when Jesus returns, the earth will quake and the Lord will stand on the Mount of Olives. The earth also quaked at the time of Jesus' Crucifixion. An earthquake fault runs through Jerusalem and under the Mount of Olives.

Louisiana Landmark

Louisiana's Supreme Court has ruled that its legislature has the right to order the teaching of creation-science whenever evolution-science is taught in the state's public elementary and secondary schools.

Millions of Tons

Millions of tons of water evaporate each day from the oceans and vegetation of the earth, then eventually condense and fall as rain. Much of this water runs back into the sea, its point of origin. Science calls this the hydrologic, or water cycle.

Scientists did not establish the evidence for a complete water cycle until the sixteenth or seventeenth century. But the Scriptures described it more than 2,000 years ago in Psalm 135:7 and Jeremiah 10:13.

Missing

The "geologic column" that evolutionists use to date fossils and rocks is found in few places on earth.

Neanderthal Man

Scientists once thought the stooped Neanderthal Man was a link between man and ape. Later analysis revealed the man simply had a bad case of rickets!

Near Fattest Redwoods

California's Hume Lake Christian Conference

Center lies only four miles from the world's largest tree. The General Grant tree, a Sequoia redwood, measures 83 feet, 2 inches in circumference.

Near Tallest Redwoods

California's Mt. Hermon Christian Conference Center stands in the middle of some of the world's tallest trees, the coastal redwoods. Adjacent Felton State Park offers picturesque walks among these towering giants.

Nearest Star

Traveling at a speed of 1,000 miles an hour, it would take three million years to reach the nearest star, Proxima Centauri.

Nebraska Man

Bone fragments once thought to be "Nebraska Man" turned out to be only a pig's tooth!

No Theory

No scientific theory exists to explain the origin of matter, space or time.

Not San Francisco's "Fault"

The infamous San Francisco earthquake of 1906, which registered 8.25 on the Richter scale, was not the most severe earthquake to hit the United States in this century. It was the Alaskan Good Friday earthquake of 1964 that registered 8.4 and destroyed downtown Anchorage.

Ocean Springs

Springs of water exist beneath the sea, particularly in the South Sea Islands and along the coasts of Greece, Italy, Israel and Syria. In 1976 the U. S. Geological Survey discovered fresh water springs off the east coast of the United States.

The book of Job, oldest book of the Bible, describes "the springs of the sea" (Job 38:16). Channels also run beneath the sea. The Bible alludes to sea channels (II Samuel 22:16), yet they are a 20th century discovery.

Old Mariner

Noah was 600 years old when he rode the churning waters of the Flood in a wooden ark.

Pathfinder of the Sea

Clues in the Bible inspired Matthew Fontaine Maury (1806-1873) to discover "the paths of the sea" and later to find natural international ocean routes that have saved shipping companies millions of dollars.

Confined to his bed during an illness, Maury had his son read to him from the Bible. One day the boy read from Psalm 8, which makes reference to "the paths of the sea" (see verse 8).

"If God said there are paths in the sea, I am going to

find them when I get out of this bed," Maury told his son.

Maury became the first to recognize the interaction of the earth's winds upon the currents of the sea. From this he reasoned that there must be paths beneath the sea that would permit ships to make better time if they took advantage of these natural undersea "routes."

From ship's logs he studied these winds and currents in detail, then plotted ship routes across the ocean that later became the basis of an international maritime agreement.

In 1923, Maury's home state of Virginia erected monuments both in Richmond and in Goshen that pay tribute to Maury's achievements and note the part the Bible played in his discoveries. The inscription on one monument reads in part:

"Matthew Fontaine Maury, pathfinder of the seas, the genius who first snatched from the ocean and atmosphere the secret of their laws .... Every mariner for countless ages, as he takes his chart to shape his course through the seas, will think of thee."

Petrified Forest

The trees in Arizona's Petrified Forest are "imported." Park officials say they probably floated into the area millions of years ago from flooding streams. They were buried under mud and sand, then covered over by layers of silica-rich volcanic ash. The silica and other minerals gradually filled in the wood cells until the logs had virtually become stone.

Is there further significance to the Petrified Forest, from a Biblical point of view? "Young earth" creationists believe so. They theorize that the timbers may have been deposited by a worldwide flood.

Piltdown Man

When in 1910 some seemingly ancient bones were found in a gravel pit near Piltdown Common, England, the scientific world rushed to proclaim the bones as clear evidence of evolution. For more than 40 years, almost every science textbook contained information about the discovery and significance of the Piltdown Man.

In 1953, the Piltdown Man was discovered to be one of the greatest hoaxes in history. Evidence suggests that the bones were no more than a human skull artificially aged with potassium bichromate and doctored with ape teeth borrowed from Oxford University's anatomy department. After the embarrassing discovery, the story of Piltdown Man was removed from science books and the educational scene.

Process Education

Horace Mann, known as the father of the American public school movement, admired Charles Darwin's writing and actively campaigned to rid this country's educational system of Christian philosophy. Mann rejected Christian conversion as a means of character development and replaced it with the evolutionary humanistic view that man can be perfected through environment and education.

Progressive Education

John Dewey, a well-known spokesman for progressive education in the early 1900's, signed the first Humanist Manifesto in 1933. In this he bluntly stated his belief that "Man is a part of nature and that he has emerged as the result of a continuous process." Dewey regarded the universe "as self-existing and not created."

Dewey was greatly influenced by Charles Darwin and led a philosophical movement called pragmatism. He is also the founder of the philosophy called instrumentalism which proposes that man must use intelligence as an instrument for overcoming any obstacles.

Sowing Seed

"Johnny Appleseed," who planted thousands of apple trees across eastern America in the early days, was also known for his distribution of religious tracts.

Sodom and Gomorrah

According to the Bible, God destroyed the cities of Sodom and Gomorrah with fire and brimstone because evil existed there. The remains of these two sites are believed to lie near or even beneath the lower end of the Dead Sea.

Some sources suggest that petroleum and gases may have ignited to cause the inferno. If God did indeed use such natural phenomenon, it was still clearly the judgment of God from "the Lord out of heaven" (see

Genesis 19:24).

Many free-standing pillars of salt are located in the area. West of the sea's southern tip lies an entire five-mile long mountain range comprised mainly of crystalline salt.

Solar System

One example of God's creativity lies in the orbits of the planets of our solar system. Venus rotates backwards rather than in the same direction that it travels around the sun. Uranus almost rolls along in its orbit at a 98 degree tilt.

The Dead Sea

The Dead Sea is 1,292 feet below sea level. It is at the lowest point of an earthquake fault that runs from Mt. Hermon, in Lebanon, to the Gulf of Aqabah.

The Embryo

Psalm 139:13-17 describes the human embryo in remarkable detail, especially when understood in the light of the Hebrew language in which the description was originally written.

Verse 16, translated, reads: "Your eyes have seen my embryo and in thy book all of my parts were recorded. All the days of my life were accounted for when as yet there were none of them."

2,000 Stars

One can see only about 2,000 stars with the naked eye but one million stars with a small telescope. With the most powerful telescope one can see about 1,000 million stars. Yet this is only a fraction of the stars that exist. There is said to be as many galaxies in the universe as stars in our galaxy.

A Record Price

A copy of the famous Gutenberg Bible brought the highest price ever paid for a printed book, says the *Guinness Book of World Records*. Texas University bought one of only 21 known complete copies for $2.4 million in 1978.

American Bible Society

The library of the American Bible Society in New York City, largest of its kind in the Western Hemisphere, contains more than 40,000 volumes of Scriptures in over 1,600 languages and dialects and includes many old, rare and historic Bibles and New Testaments.

The language chart on the first floor of the Bible House lists the names of over 1,700 languages and dialects into which the Scriptures have been translated and published since the invention of the printing press. The dates of the first New Testament and the first Bible to be published in each language are given.

Bible Museum

The Bible Museum in Eureka Springs, the Arkansas resort town, contains the largest number of old Bibles (7,000 volumes) and ancient sacred writings (3,000 primitive manuscripts) ever assembled into a single *private* collection.

Bible-Reading Marathon

In 1983, a Kiwanis Club in Amarillo, Texas sponsored a Bible-reading marathon that lasted 90 hours. Shown on local television for five days in November, the marathon featured appearances by Sen. John Tower, Sen. Lloyd Bentzen and former Dallas Cowboys quarterback Roger Staubach.

Bibles for America

The American Bible Society (ABS) was founded in 1816 to distribute Bibles on a mass basis to the American people. One of the ABS early presidents was John Jay, a former President of the Continental Congress and the first Chief Justice of the United States Supreme Court.

Christmas Surprise

Under cover of fog, George Washington crossed the Delaware on Christmas day, 1776, and caught the British enemy by surprise. Washington's superb timing and daring turned the tide in the Revolutionary War.

Early America's Supreme Court

The first Chief Justice of the United States Supreme Court, John Jay, was a devout and respected evangelical Christian of Huguenot descent who at one time served as president of the historic American Bible Society. Against the accepted common practice of his time, Chief Justice Jay bought slaves and immediately set them free.

The fourth Chief Justice of the United States, John Marshall, served for a time as an officer of the American Sunday School Union (now the American Missionary Fellowship).

Eisenhower Administration

Under the Eisenhower administration, a prayer room was established off the rotunda of the capitol. The room includes a stained glass window showing George Washington kneeling in prayer. The room is open only to congressional officials.

Government and the Bible

The first Bible printed in America—known as the Aiken Bible—was authorized by the U. S. Congress in 1781.

Government and the Church

The majority of U. S. Congress members attend church regularly, according to a 1982 survey. Most journalists, the same survey discovered, do not.

Hawaii Gets Bibles

During the 1983 "Year of the Bible" campaign, Youth With a Mission placed a Bible in each of Hawaii's 320,000 homes.

Islam

Islam is now the third largest religious force on the North American continent. There are 2.2 million Muslims in the United States.

Judeo-Christian Concepts

Until after the time of Abraham Lincoln, law in the United States rested on Judeo-Christian concepts. One of the emblems above the Supreme Court Bench is a tableau of the Ten Commandments. Moses is included among the great lawgivers in Herman A. MacNeil's marble sculpture group on the east front of the bench.

Liberty Bell

The Scriptural quotation on the Liberty Bell, taken from Leviticus 25:10, states: "Proclaim liberty throughout all the land unto all the inhabitants thereof."

The bell, first forged in England, broke as it was rung after its arrival in Philadelphia. It was recast in Philadelphia from the same metal and with the same inscription. Little did those who first cast the bell know that later it would be used against them.

Liberty or Death

Patrick Henry, known for his famous words, "Give me liberty or give me death!" shouted this cry of freedom in church—though not in a church service. The scene was St. John's Church in Richmond, Virginia, site of the second Virginia convention.

Lincoln: Prayer Day

President Abraham Lincoln held the first National Day of Prayer. By law today, two such days are allowed each year.

Motto's Origin

Treasury Secretary Salmon Chase is given the credit for putting the motto, "In God We Trust," on U. S. coins during the Civil War. But the move was prompted by a clergyman who wrote Chase: "From my heart, I have felt our national shame is in disowning God as not the least cause of our present national disorders." Chase also chose green as the color for U. S. currency.

Nativity Case

In 1984 the U. S. Supreme Court ruled that cities may sponsor Christmas displays of Nativity scenes without violating the Constitution's separation of church and state. The case that triggered the issue involved a Nativity scene owned by the city of Pawtucket, Rhode Island. The vote was 5-4, with Chief Justice Warren Burger casting the deciding vote.

National Prayer Breakfast

The National Prayer Breakfast, held each January in Washington, D. C., draws more than 3,000 guests. Sponsored by International Christian Leadership, it is by invitation only.

One Nation Under God

The Pledge of Allegiance has undergone two changes since it originally appeared in print in 1892. The original wording read, "I pledge allegiance to my flag . . . " In 1923 the phrase was expanded to read "the flag of the United States of America." In 1954, President Eisenhower added the words, "under God," to give the pledge its present form.

Prayer at State Level

All 50 state legislatures open their sessions with prayer. But in Nebraska, the practice was challenged in a case (Marsh v. Chambers) that finally went to the Supreme Court. In 1983 the high court ruled, by a 6-3 vote, that paid chaplains do not violate the separation of church and state.

Chief Justice Warren Burger called the practice "deeply embedded in the history and tradition of this country." Just three days after the first Congress authorized the appointment of paid chaplains, Burger pointed out, final agreement was reached on the language of the Bill of Rights.

"Clearly the men who wrote the First Amendment Religious Clause," wrote Burger in his decision, "did not view paid legislative chaplains and opening prayers as a violation of that amendment."

Prayer in Government

Both the U. S. Senate and the House of Representatives have an official chaplain, and Congress opens its sessions with prayer.

Presidential Oath

The President takes his oath of office with his hand upon the Bible.

President Reagan

President Reagan declared 1983 the "Year of the Bible." In his address to a gathering of the National Religious Broadcasters that same year, he said: "I'm accused of being simplistic at times with some of the problems that confront us. I've often [thought], within the covers of that single Book are all the answers to all the problems that face us today if we'd only look there. (Applause). 'The grass withereth, the flower fadeth: but the Word of our God shall stand forever.' "

President Sued

A southern California group affiliated with the American Civil Liberties Union filed suit against President Ronald Reagan for declaring 1983 the "Year of the Bible."

The courts ruled that the declaration was constitutional because it was consistent with what past Presidents have done and because Bible reading was noncompulsory.

Revolutionary War Skirmish

During a Revolutionary War skirmish, James Caldwell, a pastor and chaplain of a New Jersey regiment, took creative action when wadding for muskets ran low. He ran to a nearby Presbyterian church and grabbed a handful of *Isaac Watts Psalm Books*, yelling, "Now, boys, give them Watts!"

The incident later inspired poet/author Bret Harte to write this verse:

> . . . . They were left in the lurch
> For the want of more wadding, he
>   ran to the church,
> Broke the door, stripped the pews,
>   and dashed out in the road
> With his arm full of hymnbooks
>   and threw down his load
> At their feet. Then above all the
>   shouting and shots
> Rang his voice: "Put Watts into
>   'em! Boys, give 'em Watts."

Seal of the United States

Benjamin Franklin chose a Biblical motif for his proposed design of the United States seal. The design depicted Moses dividing the waters of the Red Sea, permitting the escape of the Israelites from Pharaoh's hot pursuit. The inscription read: "Rebellion against tyranny is obedience to God." Franklin's design was turned down, however.

Seven Signers

Seven signers of the Declaration of Independence, including Benjamin Franklin, are buried in the cemetery of Christ Church in Philadelphia. A son of William Penn is buried beneath the church's altar.

Signers of the U. S. Constitution

John Witherspoon, a one-time president of Princeton, was the only clergyman to sign the U. S. Constitution.

The Church That Took on Capone

William McCarrell had just assumed the pastorate of a church in Cicero, Illinois, near Chicago, when gangster Al Capone took over the town. Brothels and speakeasies flourished. Capone's men manhandled the mayor and shotgunned town enemies from their roaming roadsters as the townspeople stood by.

Determined to see Cicero return to law and order, McCarrell and his church soon turned the town around and even converted some of Capone's own henchmen.

In 1930, McCarrell founded the Independent Fundamental Churches of America (IFCA), now with more than 100,000 members.

The Enemy in Rout

Joshua's followers brought down the walls of Jericho by playing their trumpets, but in a slightly less miraculous event during the War of 1812, two teenage girls, Abigail and Rebecca Bates, scared off the British by playing the drum and fife.

When the girls saw a boatload of British soldiers about to land, they hid behind a lighthouse and began playing "Yankee Doodle" on their musical instruments. The soldiers turned and fled. Abigail and Rebecca Bates became immediate local heroines.

The Ride of Paul Revere

Paul Revere, of French Huguenot descent, used a borrowed horse to make his famous ride through the streets and countryside, warning the colonists of the impending British invasion.

Every year on April 18 in Boston's Old North Church, someone hangs a lantern in the belfry tower. As crowds watch, the vivid story described in the famous Longfellow poem, "The Midnight Ride of Paul Revere," is re-enacted.

The Traveler's Bible

A majority of American hotel and motel rooms have Bibles, thanks to Gideons, International, founded in 1899 in a Wisconsin hotel.

The Gideons distribute almost 23 million Bibles annually. In 1984, the 300-millionth copy of a Gideon Bible, specially bound, was given to President Ronald Reagan.

Unregistered

Nearly 15 million Christians are not registered to vote reports the National Association of Evangelicals.

Unusual Sentence

In Houston, Texas a 19-year-old girl who pleaded guilty to writing 33 bad checks was ordered by District Judge Michael McSpadden to attend church once a week for three years.

Sports and Olympics

A Matter of Ethics

Al Worthington, baseball coach for Jerry Falwell's Liberty Baptist College in Lynchburg, Virginia, once pitched for the Chicago White Sox but quit when he could not conscientiously collaborate with colleagues who were "stealing signals" from an observer in the outfield bleachers. Worthington later pitched for the Minnesota Twins.

A Star Ordained

Terry Cummings of the San Diego Clippers is an ordained minister. After recovering from a serious illness in the 1982-83 season, Cummings, formerly a DePaul University star, became a leading scorer in the National Basketball Association.

He was led to Christ by a high school teammate while a troubled teenager on Chicago's south side.

African Athletes

Azusa Pacific University sent two Nigerian athletes to the 1984 Summer Olympics. Christian Okoye has thrown the discus 194'2", and Innocent Egbunike holds the African record for the 200-meter run.

The evangelical university is located, as its name implies, in Azusa, California, a town that attained its name in a promotional campaign that promised "Everything from A to Z in USA."

Basketball and the Bible

Pat Williams, general manager of the Philadelphia

174

76ers has memorized nearly 2,000 Bible verses. "The Lord promises success," says Williams, "when one meditates on His Word. I memorize while I'm out for my daily run. It has rebuilt my thought structure. It refocuses my emotions. And it redirects my goals. I have a greater ability to concentrate."

Christian Buddies in the Fast Lane

An American quartet of black athletes ran a world record 37.86-second 400-meter relay at the World Track and Field Championships in Helsinki, Finland, in the summer of 1983. The four athletes have more in common than the public may realize. Three of the four—Willie Gault, Calvin Smith and Carl Lewis—are born-again Christians. The trio consider the Helsinki achievement not only a victory for the United States but a "spiritual victory as well."

Shortly after the achievement, Gault signed a four-year contract with the Chicago Bears.

Christian Taskforce Abroad

During the summer of 1984, teams of the evangelically oriented Athletes in Action took the gospel into more than 40 countries. In 1983, AIA teams, composed of some 270 collegiate and post-collegiate athletes, compiled a 70 percent win record in worldwide competition.

Gold Medalist

Carl Lewis, former track star at the University of

Houston who won four Gold Medals in the 1984 Summer Olympics, is active in a movement called "Lay Witnesses for Christ."

Gridiron Bible Studies

Some 40 players and staff members of the Dallas Cowboys regularly attend the Cowboys' weekly Bible class. Howard Hendricks, a professor of Christian Education at Dallas Theological Seminary, is their teacher.

Kickoff

Rafael Septien, place-kicker for the Dallas Cowboys, was the 20,000th member to join the First Baptist Church of Dallas, Texas. He was led to a knowledge of the Savior by his girlfriend who later became his wife.

Olympic Hostel

Biola University in LaMirada, California, opened its dormitories as a 3,000-bed youth hostel for Christian workers who helped to evangelize the Los Angeles Olympics' crowds. The name "Biola" is an acronym of the school's original name, The Bible Institute of Los Angeles, at one time located on Hope Street in downtown Los Angeles.

Olympic Taskforce

More than 13,000 evangelical Christian workers united to reach the Summer Olympics' crowds with the gospel. This church work involved numerous evangelical denominational groups along with such para-church organizations as Campus Crusade, Youth With a Mission, the American Bible Society, World Vision and the Moody Institute of Science. Hundreds of southern California churches also participated. Athletes from Communist nations were among those reached with the gospel.

Pastor to the President

Don Moomaw, who has been a pastor to President Reagan, was a football star at UCLA in the 1950's. He was the spiritual leader of a UCLA Campus Crusade movement that saw nine of the eleven starting UCLA football players come to the Savior.

Among Moomaw's Christian colleagues was UCLA fullback Bob Davenport, who later coached at Indiana's Taylor University and started the "Wandering Wheels" cross-country bicycle ministry.

Moomaw, whom President Reagan invited to deliver the invocation at his 1981 inauguration, took a year's leave from the pastorate of the Bel Air Presbyterian Church near Hollywood to supervise the weightlifting competition for the 1984 Summer Olympics.

Pole Vaulter

Billy Olson of Abilene Christian College (Texas) became the first vaulter in history to clear 19 feet indoors on February 4, 1983. While working his way toward the Olympics, Olson also became a Christian. Four of the United States' nine contenders for a pole

vault berth in the 1984 Olympics came from Abilene
Christian College.

Softballer Rosie Black

In more than 18 years of pitching, softballer Rosie
Black has posted some 40,000 strikeouts, over 250
perfect games, more than 750 shutouts and some 600
no-hitters. Her pitches travel up to speeds of nearly
100 miles an hour.

The blonde star of "The Queen and her Court," a
team that travels worldwide, she has pitched against
such notables as Willie Mays and Johnny Bench. Her
team has only four players, but plays nine-man teams.
Black and her players won four games straight against
Japan's major league baseball stars in the Tokyo
Giants Stadium as 30 million fans watched on
television.

All her teammates are evangelical Christians,
including her husband Paul, a near world-record
sprinter who covers the outfield.

From the outset of her career, which began at age 12,
Rosie has shared her Christian testimony over the
microphone at every game. Rosie and her family are
convinced that God has given them their sports
talents for one reason: to tell the world about
Jesus.

Vince Evans: The Teacher

In 1982, Vince Evans, quarterback for the Chicago
Bears, led his team's weekly Bible study.

States, Cities, and Towns

Abilene, Kansas

The name of Abilene, Kansas, comes from Luke 3:1. *Abilene*, in Hebrew, means "grassy plain."

Back on the Farm

In Pennsylvania's Lancaster County, visitors can spend a weekend on a farm managed by the Amish. Some 10,000 Old Order Amish populate Lancaster County. (Contact the Pennsylvania Dutch Visitors Bureau, 1799 Hempstead Road, Lancaster, PA 17601, or phone 717/299-8901.)

Capital of Gospel Music

Nashville, Tennessee, is not only the capital of country music but also the capital of gospel music. Much of today's gospel music is recorded there. In addition to its Country Music Hall of Fame, the city will soon have a Gospel Music Hall of Fame.

The city's historic Ryman Auditorium, once the home of the Grand Ole Opry, was at one time a gospel tabernacle. It was built to accommodate the preaching of Sam Jones, one of the South's most famous early evangelists, and was named after Tom Ryman, one of Jones's most illustrious converts.

Christian Retirement Community

Shell Point Village, at Fort Myers, Florida, is the world's largest Christian retirement center. It has nearly one thousand residents, its own yacht harbor, golf course and 160-bed nursing pavilion. Shell Point

Village was founded in 1968 by the Christian and Missionary Alliance.

Connecticut

The state of Connecticut was founded when a preacher led some one hundred men, women, children and a herd of cattle from the Massachusetts Bay Colony southwestward to what is now Hartford.

The preacher, Thomas Hooker, though a Puritan, disagreed with the Massachusetts Colony's autocratic government. From the pulpit of Hartford's Center Church Hooker preached a new kind of doctrine: "The foundation of authority is laid, first, in the free consent of the people."

Hooker's avant-garde ideas were incorporated into Connecticut's royal charter in 1662, and the Reverend became known as the founding father of the state.

Fort Caroline, Florida

East of Jacksonville, Florida, the National Park Service has restored Fort Caroline where French Huguenots (evangelical Protestants) landed in 1564 and established the first European colony north of Mexico.

Though fleeing religious persecution in Europe, the Huguenots encountered more difficulty in the New World. Spain saw the settlement as a threat to its new empire in the southeastern U. S. and promptly dispatched Admiral Don Pedro Menendez from St. Augustine to crush the colony.

The story, entitled "The Cross and the Sword," is

181

dramatized each year in Florida's state pageant at St. Augustine.

Hawaii

The Hawaiian Islands, which became the 50th state to join the Union on August 21, 1959, were first evangelized by American missionaries as early as 1820. But the gospel had already been planted by converts from the islands of Tahiti and Tonga who had received the gospel from British missionaries a quarter century earlier.

The Americans built on these foundations, and in their first decade on the islands they won converts in the royal family and among the chiefs, established churches, influenced legislation that upgraded moral standards, and educated thousands of children in schools. An Hawaiian "Great Awakening" erupted in Hilo in 1837, and within five years more than 37,000 converts—a fifth of the entire population—were added to the churches. Hawaii's tourist sites today include a number of places that relate directly to this early era of Christian missions.

He Owned Two States

Quaker William Penn once owned not only the entire state of Pennsylvania but also Delaware. Later Delaware separated itself from Pennsylvania in a dispute. It was never Penn's intention to name Pennsylvania after himself. King Charles II of England, to Penn's dismay, named it "Penn's Woods," from which came the name Pennsylvania.

Penn founded the state of Pennsylvania as a "Holy

Experiment." He had been deeded the land by the British government as an inheritance to settle a debt that the British owed his father. Penn, certain that God had given him this vast piece of real estate to honor Him, advertised it as far as Europe and turned it into a land of freedom for all, regardless of religious faith or nationality.

In the Capitol's Shadows

Nebraska has the nation's only nonpartisan, one-house, or unicameral, legislature. Its capitol building, an architectural masterpiece that dominates the surrounding plains, is just three blocks from the national offices of Back to the Bible Broadcast.

Jerusalem and Galilee

Two villages with Biblical names are found on the shores of Rhode Island: Jerusalem and Galilee.

Jesus in South Dakota

When Josef Meier brought his passion play from Europe to America, he chose South Dakota as its permanent site because of the terrain's similarity to the hills around Jerusalem.

Largest Ten Commandments

The largest Ten Commandments in the world are not in Israel, but on the side of a mountain in North Carolina. Located at Field of the Wood, the Ten Commandments can be read in letters carved in stone five feet high and four feet wide. These mountainside commandments are visible for miles.

Metropolis

Providence, Rhode Island, was named by Baptist Roger Williams. He was given the land free by the Indians and therefore considered it a "providence" of God.

Nineveh

The Biblical city of Nineveh, to which Jonah fled, had a population estimated to be almost the size of San Francisco, California, (678,000).

Oldest Street in America

Huguenot Street, in New Paltz, New York, is the oldest street in America. The Huguenots, who founded the town in 1677, were evangelical French Protestants who underwent much early persecution for their Christian faith.

Oregon

Evangelical Christians played a major role in the settlement of Oregon. Methodist missionaries Jason and Daniel Lee entered Oregon's Willamette Valley in the 1830's. They were so impressed with this "land of Canaan" that they promoted it to citizens in the East, eventually drawing hundreds of settlers to the region via the long boat trip around Cape Horn.

Later when Marcus and Narcissa Whitman were

murdered, along with others, at their mission station north of the Columbia River, the United States government hastily established Oregon as a territory to bring this wilderness under law. Oregon entered the Union in 1859 as the 33rd state.

Petra

One hundred miles south and east of Jerusalem, in a remote narrow canyon with nearly vertical walls, lies the ancient city of Petra, once the wealthy capital of Edom.

At one time Petra controlled caravan routes over which treasures from Arabia and the Far East were carried to Greek markets. Petra's wealthy citizens had beautiful tombs and temples, even a large amphitheater, all chiseled into the rose-red rock cliffs surrounding the city. The city appeared impregnable.

But wealth brought sin, and Jeremiah pronounced judgment upon it (Jeremiah 14:16-17). Today Petra is deserted. In the canyon city that seemed forever safe, weeds grow in the courts of its once lavish temples and palaces. It is just as the Bible foretold.

Rhode Island

The foundations of Rhode Island were planted in 1636 by Roger Williams, the same man who established the first Baptist church in America. Williams, a minister, founded Providence as the capital with the basic premise of religious and political freedom. Rhode Island became a state in 1790 (one of the original 13) and although it is the smallest of the 50 states, the church Williams planted has become the largest in America. Today more than 25 million Americans call themselves Baptist.

Solvang

Solvang, a picturesque Danish village in the Santa Ynez Valley north of Santa Barbara, California, began as the dream of a Danish Lutheran minister who announced to his church congregation in Michigan in 1910 plans to establish a Danish colony on the west coast. Another Lutheran pastor helped choose the site and arrange the purchase of 9,000 acres.

Tyre

The ships of the famous Phoenician city of Tyre once sailed as far as Spain and the British Isles. And the city was a major force during the time of Solomon. But the destruction of this powerful city was foretold by Ezekiel. Even its dusty remains, Ezekiel said in chapter 26, would be scraped off, making it bare like the top of a rock. It would become a place only for fishermen to spread nets.

From 587-574 B. C. Nebuchadnezzar beseiged the city, eventually destroying it. But wealthier residents fled to a small island a half mile off the coast where they set up ingenious defenses. With a superb navy and complex underwater obstacles, they frustrated even Alexander the Great for seven months. But finally, in 332 B. C., Alexander built a causeway to the island so that his army could attack. For material, he used stones and timber from the old city on shore. He scraped the dust from the city's ruins and threw it into the sea.

Thus the rest of the prophecy was fulfilled. The site became as bare as a rock, and today fishermen still spread their nets there to dry.

Wheat Pioneers

Kansas owes its reputation as leader of the nation's wheat production to evangelical Christians. Devout Mennonites from Russia introduced Turkey Red wheat, a hardy strain, to the land that made Kansas the "Breadbasket of the Nation." A "Wheat Palace" at Goessel, Kansas, pays tribute to these early Christian immigrants and displays a replica of the Liberty Bell—made of wheat!

Wycliffe and U. S. Tribes

Wycliffe Bible Translators has not confined its linguistic work to distant tribes on other continents. Wycliffe workers have already translated the Bible into Navajo and are at work among other American Indian tribes as well, including the Cheyenne Indians of Wyoming.

Tourist Attractions

Bible Parade

The southeastern Kansas town of Humboldt, population 2,500, holds an annual "Biblesta Parad." Floats move down the main street, school marching bands play, and folks come from miles around. The parade has only one theme: the Bible.

Every float entered by churches, clubs, and civic groups must tell a story from the Bible. Each float usually carries a Scripture verse. No one on a float wins a prize without a Biblical costume.

After the parade, town churches feed the crowds with nearly three-quarters of a ton of ham and navy beans.

Chicago

The ferris wheel originated at the 1893 World's Fair (Columbian Exposition) in Chicago. At that same fair, evangelist Dwight L. Moody mobilized Chicago's evangelical forces and reached two million people with the gospel message.

Christian Guest Ranch

What was once an executive retreat for Phillips Oil Company near Kremmling, Colorado, southeast of Steamboat Springs, has become a Christian resort. Lichen Guest Ranch, which has a 110-acre lake, can house over 200 guests.

Church on Rails

In the early days, Sunday Schools were sometimes

held in railroad cars. At one time seven "chapel cars," each with a pastor or missionary family living inside, traveled across America, stopping for a few days at a time in small towns along the way. A car would be put on a sidetrack, then picked up later to be pulled to the next town. Two of these "chapel cars" can still be seen today, one at Green Lake, Wisconsin, the other at the museum of Prairie Village near Madison, South Dakota.

Famous Newscarriers

At the Freedoms Foundation at Valley Forge, Pennsylvania, where George Washington's troops withstood a bitter winter, visitors can wander through an exhibit of photos of famous Americans who began their careers as newsboys.

Freedom Trail "Beaver"

Along the Freedom Trail in Boston, Massachusetts, one can board a replica of the ship "Beaver," made famous by the Boston Tea Party, and toss a carton of tea overboard.

Great Americans

Since the turn of the century more than 100 men and women have been named to "The Hall of Fame for Great Americans" in New York City. Of these, five have been theologians or preachers including evangelist Jonathan Edwards and Roger Williams, America's early champion of religious freedom and founder of the first Baptist church in America.

Until 1970, voting for candidates for the Hall of Fame took place very five years, but now it is every three. To be voted in, one must have been dead at least 25 years and receive a majority of the electoral votes cast. No clergyman has been added since 1910. Those receiving scattered votes, however, have included Adoniram Judson, the first Baptist missionary to Burma. Judson received votes in every election through 1930, but has received none since then.

Jefferson Memorial

Words inscribed inside the Jefferson Memorial stress that God is the ultimate author of freedom. Says Jefferson, "God who gave us life gave us liberty. Can the liberties of a nation be secure when we have removed a conviction that these liberties are the gift of God?"

Jerusalem Gate

The "Golden Gate" in Jerusalem's East Wall stands on the foundation stones of the portal that Jesus triumphantly entered a few days before He was crucified.

Six hundred years earlier, the prophet Ezekiel had prophesied that the Messiah would enter through this gate. But Ezekiel also said that the gate would be closed:

"Then said the Lord unto me, This gate shall be shut, it shall not be opened, and no man shall enter in by it; because the Lord, the God of Israel, hath entered in by it, therefore it shall be shut" (Ezekiel 44:2).

For centuries much of this prophecy had little meaning. But in 1543, Sultan Suleiman the Magnificent did a strange thing. He restored the gate with its arches and ornaments. Then, because the road from the Kidron Valley up to the gate had deteriorated, he immediately had the gate walled up with blocks of stone. It still remains sealed.

Jesus on the Mountain Top

A gigantic statue called "Christ of the Ozarks" atop Magnetic Mountain at Eureka Springs, Arkansas, stands seven stories high. Arms outstretched, the statue measures 65 feet from fingertip to fingertip and weighs more than one million pounds. The figure was built to withstand 500 mile-an-hour winds. An automobile could be suspended from either wrist without affecting the statue.

Lincoln Memorial

The words of Abraham Lincoln inscribed in stone inside the Lincoln Memorial refer to "God," the "Bible," "providence," "the Almighty," and "divine attributes." Lincoln also quotes Psalm 19:9: "As was said 3000 years ago so it still must be said, 'The judgments of the Lord are true and righteous altogether.' "

Little-Known Fact

Mary McLeod Bethune (1875-1955), Negro educator honored by a statue in Washington, D. C., at one time studied at Chicago's Moody Bible Institute. She was named "Mother of the Century" by the Dorie Miller Foundation in 1954.

Monument to a Haystack

Ripley's "Believe It or Not" cites a structure at Williamstown, Massachusetts, that it calls "the world's only monument to a haystack."

But there is more to the story. In 1806, five evangelical students at Williams College had gathered in a maple grove to pray for revival. A sudden thunderstorm drove them into the shelter of a nearby haystack where they prayed fervently for world evangelism. The sun burst through the clouds, and the students left convinced God would use their lives in a dramatic way.

From this small band of students came a great surge in missionary interest and some of the greatest missionaries of all time including: Samuel J. Mills, Luther Rice and Adoniram Judson.

Most Complete Collection

The nation's most complete collection of coins from Biblical times and countries is located in the rotunda of Christus Gardens in Gatlinburg, Tennessee.

Northwest Missionary

A statue of missionary Marcus Whitman, Bible in hand, stands inside the Washington state capitol. Whitman and his wife, Narcissa, the first white woman to cross the Rockies, evangelized Indians near what is now Walla Walla, Washington, before they and more than a dozen others were massacred at their mission station in 1847. The tragedy prompted Congress to bring law to the Northwest wilderness and establish the Oregon Territory.

Old North Church

An exact replica of the Old North Church, where Americans hung a lantern to warn of British attack, stands on the Forest Lawn Cemetery grounds in Glendale, California.

Parthenon in Nashville

A remarkable replica of the Parthenon stands in Nashville, Tennessee. It is the exact size of the original Parthenon in Athens, Greece, which the Apostle Paul could view so well as he delivered his famous sermon on Mars Hill. (See Acts 17.) Nashville has often been called the "Athens of the South."

Plymouth "Mayflower"

At Plymouth, Massachusetts, tourists can board a replica of the "Mayflower" that brought the early Pilgrims to America. Visitors usually come away amazed at how 102 passengers could have crowded into such small quarters for the long transoceanic trip.

Rocky Mountain Lodge

At Jackson, Wyoming, a ranch once operated by Youth for Christ is now a privately owned Christian outreach called Rocky Mountain Lodge and Outfitters. It specializes in giving church youth groups a superb week-long adventure in the Grand Tetons. Solid Bible study is also a part of the program.

San Francisco

At the 1939 Golden Gate Exposition in San Francisco, an evangelical pastor blended the gospel with unique scientific demonstrations and drew record crowds. Irwin Moon fried eggs on a cold stove, started light bulbs with his bare fingers and altered his voice with whiffs of a helium-oxygen mixture.

From this success later came the Moody Institute of Science which Moon founded in 1945. Millions of people since then have seen Moody science films and demonstrations at world's fairs from New York and Seattle to San Antonio and Montreal where these films were the longest running exhibits. Moody science films are seen by a half million people daily around the world.

Sing on Grandfather Mountain

On the fourth Sunday of every June, thousands gather high on Grandfather Mountain near Linville, North Carolina, for the "Singing on the Mountain Gospel Festival." The event originated more than a half century ago as the "Hartley family reunion" but then grew into a free public event. Governors and celebrities sometimes come, and some years the Festival has drawn as many as 50,000. Some families come several nights early and camp out in nearby McRea Meadows where they enjoy gospel singing around their tents and campfires.

Statue of Liberty

After holding high the torch of freedom for nearly a century, the Statue of Liberty finally had to undergo arm repair. Workmen thought they would have to remove the arm to overhaul the gallant lady for her 100th anniversary in 1986. But they were able to make the repair without such drastic measures.

When French sculptor Frederic Auguste Bartholdi designed the Statue of Liberty, he used his mother as the model. The statue's iron framework, however, was designed by Gustav Eiffel. His most famous work is the Eiffel Tower in Paris.

Sunday School Founder

A statue in honor of Robert Raikes, the Englishman who founded the Sunday School movement, stands in the city of Toronto, Canada. The Sunday School originated in Gloucester, England, in 1780. It first appeared in the United States in 1785 when William Elliot began a Sunday School in his home in Virginia. The first church-located Sunday School, according to some authorities, was planted by John Wesley in Savannah, Georgia.

Walls of Jerusalem in Arkansas

A replica of the Old Jerusalem Wall, under construction in Eureka Springs, Arkansas, is being built to the exact specifications of the original wall: five stories high. Real camels often can be seen near.

Washington Monument

Those people who climb the 879 steps of the Washington Monument will find a number of Scripture verses at landings along the way. The elevator makes the ascent in only 70 seconds.

For more than 25 years the Washington Monument, today 555 feet high, stood only 150 feet tall. A political quarrel held up further construction.

The Washington Monument sinks an average of six inches a year.

Whitefield at Penn

A statue of evangelist George Whitefield stands on the University of Pennsylvania campus. When Whitefield came to Philadelphia, Benjamin Franklin, who greatly admired the evangelist, decided this "outdoor preacher" needed a building in which to deliver his sermons. So he helped raise money for the edifice. It later became the first building on what is now the University of Pennsylvania.

Wycliffe Museum

The campus of the Summer Institute of Linguistics (SIL), an affiliate of Wycliffe Bible Translators, is an adjunct campus of the University of Texas at Arlington, as well as home for the international academic offices of SIL. The complex includes a newly-opened Museum of Anthropology, designed to help students and the public at large understand the cultures of the world.

INDEX

Index

Index

Index

Index